History of the TOWN OF HINGHAM
Plymouth County
Massachusetts

Solomon Lincoln, Jr.

HERITAGE BOOKS
2014

HERITAGE BOOKS
AN IMPRINT OF HERITAGE BOOKS, INC.

Books, CDs, and more—Worldwide

For our listing of thousands of titles see our website
at
www.HeritageBooks.com

A Facsimile Reprint
Published 2014 by
HERITAGE BOOKS, INC.
Publishing Division
5810 Ruatan Street
Berwyn Heights, Md. 20740

Originally published
Hingham:
Caleb Gill, Jr. and Farmer and Brown
1827

— Publisher's Notice —
In reprints such as this, it is often not possible to remove blemishes from the original. We feel the contents of this book warrant its reissue despite these blemishes and hope you will agree and read it with pleasure.

International Standard Book Numbers
Paperbound: 978-0-7884-0434-4
Clothbound: 978-0-7884-9012-5

PREFACE.

My design in the compilation of the following pages, has been to collect such facts relating to the settlement, subsequent history, and present state of the town of Hingham, as appeared to be worthy of preservation. The consideration that many of these facts were preserved only by tradition, or recorded in the decaying leaves of public and private records, rendered it desirable that an opportunity should be embraced to preserve them in a more durable form. Nearly two centuries have elapsed since this town was settled, and no full sketch of its history has ever been published. I have been desirous of noticing such individuals as have been distinguished in public or private life, and especially those of whom only traditionary information is preserved—and that fast fading from the memory of our aged fathers. It has been my endeavour to be scrupulously correct; but it will not be remarkable, if some errours in deciphering ancient manuscripts and in copying our town records (some portions of which have become almost illegible,) should have escaped me.

There may be much of this history, which, to some readers, will appear uninteresting, and perhaps some portions of it may be thought too trifling and unimportant to be given to the public. The consideration that we search with avidity for almost any facts which are rendered interesting solely on account of their antiquity, and that "the trifles of the present age become matters of weight with future generations," is a sufficient reason for the introduction of facts of this description.

While engaged in collecting the materials, I have been indebted to many gentlemen in this and other towns, for the readiness with which they have attended to my inquiries for information, and for the kindness with which they have loaned to me valuable manuscripts which have been of essential service to me in endeavouring to illustrate the early history of the town. I feel under particular obligations to Hon. JAMES SAVAGE, for the politeness with which he has furnished information from the public records in Boston, and for the loan of the manuscripts of the late JAMES OTIS LINCOLN; and to JOTHAM LINCOLN, Esq. Town Clerk of Hingham, for his unwearied patience in furnishing whatever I have desired from the town records. Other gentlemen, to whom I am indebted for much genealogical and traditionary information, will, I hope, find a sufficient acknowledgement of their kindness in the notes.

Influenced by no other motive but that of wishing to preserve for the gratification of the inhabitants of Hingham, whatever is worthy of preservation in the history of the town, or in the character of individuals, I trust that any imperfections will be regarded with candour; and shall think myself richly compensated for the time which I have devoted to the subject, if my readers can find any thing in the result of my labours, productive of instruction or amusement.

S. LINCOLN, JR.

HINGHAM, December 1st, 1827.

HISTORY OF HINGHAM.

HINGHAM, a Post Town, in the County of Plymouth, Massachusetts, has the Bay, North,—Cohasset, East,—Scituate and Abington, South, and Weymouth, West. The greatest extent of the town from North to South, is seven miles and three quarters, and from East to West, about five miles—containing 13,775 square acres. The original limits of Hingham embraced the present town of Cohasset, which was set off and incorporated April 26, 1770. Until March 26, 1793, Hingham formed a part of Suffolk County; at that time, it was annexed to the new County of Norfolk. By an act of the Legislature, passed June 20, 1793, repealing the former act, so far as it related to Hingham and Hull, Hingham again became a part of the County of Suffolk; and by an act passed June 18th, 1803, Hingham was annexed to the County of Plymouth, of which it now forms a part. The distance from Hingham to Plymouth is 26 miles, and from Hingham to Boston, about 14 miles by land, and between 12 and 13 by water.

SURFACE, SOIL, PRODUCTIONS, &c. A considerable portion of this town is of an uneven surface. The northern section of the settlement, is principally in a valley, between continued elevations of land, generally of easy ascent, but sometimes abrupt and rocky. Leaving the northerly section, and following the main road to Plymouth, we ascend to a higher and level tract of land, called the "Lower Plain." Leaving the "Lower Plain," we soon ascend again to high and level land, called "Glad Tidings Plain;" still higher and farther south, is "Liberty Plain." In the north part of the town, near the sea shore, there are several beautiful eminences, which afford excellent views of the metropolis of the State and its environs, of Boston Harbour, and of the adjacent country. The highest elevation of land is at Prospect Hill, in the southerly part of the town; and the next highest is at Turkey Hill, in the easterly part. Baker's,* Otis's,† Squirrel and Pleasant Hills, in the north part of the town, command extensive and delightful prospects. The land at Hockley Fields, and in the western part of the town, has a beautifully undulating surface.

The soil, is in many parts of the town, rich and productive. North of the main road from Hingham Bridge at the Back River, to Cohasset, (except at the eastern part,) the soil is uncommonly fertile, and produces abundant crops of grass, grain and vegetables, with the application of comparatively little labour. There is also, excellent land in the north-easterly part of the town, and upon the Plains; in the south-westerly and westerly parts the soil is lighter, and best calculated for grazing. In the southerly and easterly sections, there are extensive tracts of valuable woodland abounding with the pine, the oak, the

* Baker's Hill derives its name from Nicholas and Nathaniel Baker who settled at its foot.
† Otis's Hill takes its name from John Otis, one of the first settlers of the town. Its original name was Weary-all Hill, on account of the abruptness of its ascent on the south side.

maple and the walnut. There are many enterprizing and good farmers, whose skill and industry are richly rewarded. Considerable attention is paid to the cultivation of fruit trees, but the productions of the soil are not sufficient to supply the wants of the inhabitants.

Mechanical and mercantile pursuits have of late, attracted more attention than agriculture. In 1820, the number of persons engaged in agriculture, was 279, and in commerce and manufactures 540.

STREAMS AND POND. The only considerable collection of fresh water is *Accord Pond*, in the south part of the town. It is situated partly in Hingham, Abington, and Scituate. The principal stream of water which flows through the town, originates from this pond—it is called *Wear River*.* A small brook which flows from the west part of the town, and empties into the Mill Pond at the Harbour, it is said, attracted the attention of the first inhabitants and induced them to settle in the valley through which it flows. *Weymouth Back River*, a navigable stream, separates Hingham from Weymouth. A bridge was thrown across this stream, in 1812, by the Hingham and Quincy Bridge and Turnpike Corporation.

ISLANDS. Within the limits of Hingham, there are five small islands, viz. : Bumkin, Chandler's (sometimes called Langley's,) Ragged, Sailor's (sometimes called Sarah's,) and Button island. Bumkin island, the largest and most valuable, is situated without the harbour, the others are within the harbour.

MANUFACTURES, TRADE AND COMMERCE. There are in Hingham, two manufactories of woollens—three grist mills—one furnace for the casting of hollow and other

---

* Wear River takes its name from the fact that a *wear* was erected in this river to take alewives. The town authorized Thomas Loring, Clement Bates, Nicholas Jacob, and Joseph Andrews to erect a *wear* for that purpose, in 1637.

iron ware,—one brass foundry—several-tanneries—one rope-walk—salt works—one saw-mill—a printing office—book store—and an extensive manufactory of umbrellas, &c.* In addition to these, there is the usual variety of mechanics to be found in most towns of a similar size, viz. : iron smiths, silver smiths, wheelwrights, plough-makers, pump and block makers, sail makers, coopers, book-binders, cabinet and chair makers, saddle, harness and trunk makers, hat manufacturers, a clock maker, bakers, &c.

There is also, a large number of traders in English, American and West India goods.

There is but one Hotel, which is near the centre of the North Village. At the Harbour is a Ship Yard, in which one or more vessels are annually built.†

The shipping of the place is mostly employed in the cod and mackerel fishery,‡ and in the lumber trade and other coastwise navigation. There are four convenient Packets, which ply regularly between Hingham and Boston, for the transportation of passengers and goods.

* In the " Hingham Umbrella Manufactory," there are made annually, about 25,000 umbrellas and parasols. The number of persons employed is from 35 to 40. Mr. Benjamin S. Williams, superintendant.

† William Pitts had liberty from the selectmen to build ships and other vessels at Konohasset (Cohasset) in 1675 ; and J. Blane in 1693 had permission " to build a vessel or two near the mill."—*Town Records.*

‡ Since the year 1815, there has been the number of *one hundred and fifty-nine thousand, seven hundred and thirty-five* barrels of mackerel packed in this town. The year 1817 is not included in the estimate ; the number of barrels packed in that year not being known. These mackerel were all assorted into Nos. 1, 2, and 3—and the same Nos. are usually carried to the same markets each year. Nos. 1 are principally taken to Philadelphia—2 to the Southern States, and 3 to the West India Islands.

There are about forty sail of vessels owned in this place, chiefly employed in this business ; and their trips are from one to six weeks, as the weather and their *fortunes* may be. The vessels average

HISTORY OF HINGHAM.   9

POPULATION. In 1765, Hingham (including Cohasset) contained a population of 2467 souls. In 1800, the population of Hingham alone was 2112, viz. : Males 951 ; Females 1121 ; Coloured people 40. In 1810 the whole population was 2382. The following is a view of the census of 1820 :

Males under 10 yrs.	378	Females	367
10 to 16 "	218		195
16 " 26 "	256		258
26 " 45 "	293		339
45 and upwards	225		333
	1370		1492
			1370

			2862
Foreigners not naturalized,			10
Engaged in agriculture,			279
" " commerce,			153
" " manufactures,			387
Coloured people of both sexes,			45
First Parish,	1511	R. Polls	403
Second "	552	" "	154
Third Society,	602	" "	129
Others,	197	" "	64
Total,	2862		750
Census in 1810,	2382		
Gain in 10 years,	480.		

from six to ten hands each. The following table will show the number of sail, and the amount of barrels packed each year.

	No. sail,	No. bbls.		No. sail.	No. bbls.
1815,	14	3615	1822,	36	18631
1816,	20	6139	1823,	38	14802
1818,	25	6642	1824,	41	24457
1819,	30	11480	1825,	43	31109
1820,	30	13431	1826,	46	18554
1821,	27	10875			

The quantity of salt used in *striking* and *packing* the above mentioned number of barrels of mackerel, was 199,667 bushels.— *Hingham Gazette, Feb. 9, 1827.*

1*

The present number of qualified voters is about 550 ; and of families, 600. The town is undoubtedly as flourishing as it has been at any former period, and if the increase of population since 1820, has been in the same ratio, as for the 10 years previous, the present population of the town would amount to 3200 souls.

The actual number of polls assessed, was, in 1815, 514 ; in 1820, 547, and in 1826, 628.

MILITIA. There are in Hingham, three standing companies of militia, commanded by Capt. Charles Shute, Capt. Joshua Humphrey, and Capt. Alfred C. Hersey. There is also an excellent corps of Riflemen, called the Hingham Rifle Company. This company received its charter in 1812. The commanders of the company have been the following gentlemen, viz. :

    Capt. Duncan M. B. Thaxter,* (resigned.)
    Capt. Jairus Sprague, (resigned.)
    Capt. Laban Hersey, Jr. (promoted.)
    Capt. Charles Lane, (promoted.)

The present officers are Lieutenant, James Stephenson, Jr. Ensign, Benjamin Thomas, Jr. ; the office of Captain being vacant on account of the promotion of Capt. Lane to the office of Major.

FIRE ENGINES, &c. There are in this town four Engines for its security against fires. Fifteen men are attached to each engine. The companies are supplied with fire hooks, ladders, &c. &c.

A considerable number of the citizens have formed a Society for mutual relief in case of fires.

INSURANCE COMPANY. The Hingham Mutual Fire Insurance Company was incorporated March 4, 1826,

---

* Capt. Thaxter, was a liberal, intelligent, enterprising, and valuable citizen. He died Feb. 4, 1822, and was interred with masonic and military honours.

for the purpose of Mutual Insurance against losses by fire. It is now in successful operation.

The present officers of the company are the following, viz. :

   Jotham Lincoln, President,
   David Whiton, Treasurer,
   David Harding, Secretary,

Directors, Elijah D. Wild, Thomas Loud, John Beal, Benjamin Thomas, Moses Sprague, Jr. and Ezekiel Fearing.

SOCIETY OF MUTUAL AID, &c. The *Society of Mutual Aid* was formed by a large number of gentlemen, for the purpose of assisting each other in the recovery of *any property* that may be stolen from a member of the society —and for the detection of thieves. The society has a fund, for the promotion of the objects of its institution. The officers are a clerk, and a standing committee. The present clerk is Mr. David Andrews.

AGRICULTURAL SOCIETY. The Hingham Agricultural Society was formed in March, 1814. The society has a small library of books relating to agricultural subjects. The present officers are as follows, viz. :

   Solomon Jones, President,
   James Stephenson, Vice President,
   John Beal, Secretary,
   Benjamin Andrews, Treasurer.

LODGE. Old Colony Lodge of Free Masons, was chartered A. L. 5792, Dec. 9. Its original location was at Hanover. It was removed to Hingham A. L. 5807. This Lodge is in a flourishing state. The members have a small library of valuable books. The officers chosen in December last, were as follows, viz. :

   Fearing Loring, Master,
   Charles Fearing, Senior Warden,

Charles Gill, Junior Warden,
Elijah Lincoln, Treasurer,
David Harding, Secretary,
Asa Fuller, Marshal,
Benjamin Studley, Senior Deacon,
John Lane, Junior Deacon,
Hezekiah Lincoln, Senior Steward,
Henry Hapgood, Junior Steward.

NEWSPAPER. The only newspaper ever published in Hingham, is the *Hingham Gazette.* It was established in January of the present year. The publishers are *Jedidiah Farmer* and *Simon Brown.*

DEBATING SOCIETY. This institution was formed in 1823, by those young men of Hingham, who were attached to the political principles of the distinguished patriot and statesman, Thomas Jefferson, for the purpose of acquiring " general and political information." The society holds monthly meetings for the discussion of questions proposed by the government of the society. The members celebrate the anniversary of its institution on the Fourth of March, by a public address. Addresses to the members of the society are delivered every quarter. The government of the society consists of a President, Vice President, Treasurer, Secretary, and a Standing Committee. The Presidents of the Society have been, Messrs. David Harding, Jacob H. Loud, and Albert Fearing. The present officers are, as follows, viz. :

President, John Kingman,
Vice President, Caleb Gill, Jr.
Treasurer, John Leavitt, Jr.
Secretary, Solomon Lincoln, Jr.

Standing Committee, Elijah Lincoln, Ebed Ripley, and Enoch Whiting. The number of members is about 80.

LIBRARIES. There are in Hingham four Social Libraries owned by proprietors, one masonic, a circulating library, and a small one belonging to the agricultural society. They contain an aggregate of about 1800 volumes.

The First Social Library was formed in 1771, and contains between three and four hundred volumes of valuable books, chiefly Histories, Biographies, Travels, &c.

The Second Social Library was formed in 1773, as the preamble to the constitution of the proprietors, expresses, " for the promotion of Knowledge, Religion and Virtue, the three grand ornaments of human nature."

The Social Library of the Third Parish, recently formed, contains about 350 volumes of valuable books of History, Biography, Morality, and Fiction.

The Circulating Library owned by Mr. Caleb Gill, Jr. contains upwards of 500 volumes, principally new and interesting publications. These in addition to several valuable private libraries, afford great facilities for the acquisition of learning, to those who have any inclination for literary improvement. The favourable influence which such institutions exert over the best interests of the community can scarcely be estimated. A love of letters is frequently excited by these means of improvement, of which every individual can avail himself. The tone of manners is improved—talents cherished—and information extended in every class of the community.

Poor. Ample provision is made by the town for the relief of the poor. A spacious Alms House was erected in 1817, at an expense of upwards of four thousand dollars. The greatest part of the expense of building this house was defrayed from the proceeds of the sale of lands belonging to the town. The number of poor persons supported in the Alms House, is about 40. In addition to these, others out of the house, are relieved, who are not entirely dependant on the town for support. Beside the income arising from the labour of those in the Alms House, the average sum of money expended for the support of the poor is about $1200.

TOWN EXPENSES. The amount of money raised by tax, to defray the annual expenses, has been for several years previous to the present year, $4,000. For 1827, the amount raised was increased to $4,500. The town has also an income of considerable amount from other sources, such as the labour of the poor and from real estate. The Poor and School Fund, also, affords a considerable income, which is appropriated to the maintenance of Schools, and the support of the Poor. This fund was derived from the sale of lands which were granted to the town in 1780. The amount of money in this fund, was, on the first of January last, $3926,19 ; and the amount of notes bearing interest at four per cent. and payable in a limited time, was $3005,53, making an available fund of nearly seven thousand dollars.

The amount of money paid to teachers of schools annually, is nearly $1800—for the support of the poor, $1200.

In addition to the money raised, another tax is annually assessed, by a vote of the town, for the repair of Highways, Bridges, &c. to be paid in labour. This tax in 1825, exceeded $1700 ; in 1826, it was $1232,84, and for the present year it is $1301,78.

EDUCATION. The inhabitants of Hingham, were, at a very early date, attentive to the interests of education. The value of Free Schools, " those invaluable political and moral institutions,—our own blessing, and the glory of our fathers," appears to have been fully understood and properly appreciated by them. That they have been liberally supported in Hingham for a great length of time, is highly honourable to the character of the town ; and without the fear of subjecting himself to the charge of undue partiality to the place of his nativity, the author is free to express the opinion that the effects of good education may be discovered in the general intelligence of the citizens, and that they have been particularly conspicuous in the character of those, who, aided by the advantages of an education obtained in our common schools, have risen to elevated stations in society, and conferred honour upon the place of their nativity. The number of persons, natives of the town, who have received the advantages of a collegiate education, is large ; and unquestionably, in many instances, the first impulse towards the attainment of it, was received in our free schools. Schools for private instruction have, also, for many years, been numerous and liberally patronized. For the prosecution of the studies preparatory to a collegiate education, the munificent endowment of an academy, by Mrs. Derby, affords every facility, at a trifling expense.

Some account of the establishment of Derby Academy, may not be uninteresting to the citizens. MRS. SARAH DERBY,* by a Deed of Lease and Release, executed Oct. 21, 1784, conveyed to the persons therein named, as Trustees, the piece of land on which the Academy now stands,—with the buildings then standing thereon,—the rents and profits of which were to be appropriated, by the trustees, for the maintenance of a school in the North Parish, in Hingham, for the instruction of the youth, in such arts, languages and sciences as are therein particularly mentioned, &c.

The Trustees obtained an act of incorporation, Nov.

* Mrs. Derby's maiden name was Langley. She married Dr. Ezekiel Hersey, and after his decease, Mr. Derby of Salem. She survived her husband, and died June 17, 1790, aged 76.

11, 1784, establishing a school, called in honour of its founder, DERBY SCHOOL. The first board of Trustees was composed of the following gentlemen, viz. :

Rev. Ebenezer Gay, D. D. of Hingham,
" Daniel Shute, D. D. of Hingham,
Col. John Thaxter, of Hingham,
Hon. Benjamin Lincoln, of Hingham,
" Cotton Tufts, of Weymouth,
" Richard Cranch, of Braintree,
" William Cushing, of Scituate,
" Nathan Cushing, of Scituate,
John Thaxter, Esq. of Haverhill, and
Benjamin Lincoln, Esq. of Boston.

By an act of the Legislature, passed June 19, 1797, the *Derby School* was erected into an Academy by the name of DERBY ACADEMY.

By the Deed of Lease and Release, the school was required to be maintained and supported, for the instruction of all such males as should be admitted therein, "*in the Latin, Greek, English, and French languages, and in the sciences of Mathematics and Geography.*" And all such females as should be admitted therein, "*in writing, and in the English and French languages, arithmetic, and the art of needlework in general.*" Immediately after Mrs. Derby's decease, the Trustees were required " to elect and appoint a Preceptor for the said school, skilled in the art of writing, in the sciences aforesaid, and in the Latin, Greek, and English languages, and the sciences of mathematics, and geography ;" and also " a sensible and discreet woman skilled in the art of needle-work, whose business it shall be to instruct therein, the females that shall be admitted."

The pupils to be admitted were, " such males of the North Parish, from twelve years old and upwards, whose parents, guardians, or patrons may desire the same. And at any age under twelve years, when any male is intended for an admission to Harvard College, at the discretion of the Trustees."

The Trustees were authorized to send, each, two scholars to the school, one of each sex, of the ages and descriptions before mentioned.

Male pupils from the South Parish, intended for Harvard College are to be admitted under twelve years of age, and such others of the same Parish " as desire to be instructed in the art of surveying, navigation, and their attendant branches of the mathematics, at the request of parents, guardians or patrons." Each pupil is required to furnish a proportional share of fire-wood, under the direction of the Trustees. " And no person except such as is above mentioned and described, shall on any pretence be even admitted to the said school, unless the number of female scholars in the said school be less than thirty, or the number of males be less than forty, in either of which cases the said Trustees, their survivors or successors may admit such a number as shall increase the number of female scholars to thirty, and the number of male to forty, *preference forever to be given to such poor orphans whose guardians or patrons shall request their admittance.*"

In case it became necessary to rebuild the house, it was required to be situated central to the North Parish, as near as may be.

An annual lecture by " some able minister of the gospel" is to be delivered in the North Parish, for which he is to receive the sum of six pounds. In case of the decease of a Trustee, the survivors are authorized to fill the vacancy, and not more than four of the Trustees can be residents of Hingham.

By her Will, Mrs. Derby bequeathed to the Trustees, £2500 in Massachusetts State notes, the interest thereof to be by them appropriated for the use of the Preceptor; and £700 in silver, the interest of which, to be by them appropriated for the use of the Preceptress for the time being. She also directed that her clock and portrait should be placed in the school; and after making other legacies, created the Trustees residuary legatees of all her estate real and personal. She also expressed her desire that Abner Lincoln should be appointed Preceptor of the school as soon as opened.

In the Codicil to her Will, there was a provision inserted, that if the Trustees should neglect at any time, for the space of two years together, to apply the rents, and income of the funds to the purposes for which they were intended, they were to become the property of the President and Fellows of Harvard College, in trust, the interest thereof to be appropriated for the support of the Professor of Anatomy and Physic. She also expressed in this Codicil, her wish for the Trustees to relinquish the privilege of sending two scholars each.

I have thus enumerated the most important provisions of the Deed, Will and Codicil, that they may be fully understood by the people of Hingham, and that the liberality of the benevolent founder of the Academy may be properly appreciated.

The munificent grants and bequests of Mrs. Derby, constituted a very respectable fund, which was increased by the Legislature, by an act passed June 18, 1803, granting to the Trustees a half township of land in Maine, to be disposed of by them for the interest and benefit of the institution.

The available funds of the Academy exclusive of the building for the schools, amount at the present time, to

$24,500. The present large and commodious edifice for the use of the schools, &c. was erected in 1818.

The following named gentlemen have been the Preceptors of the School and Academy since its establishment. Abner Lincoln, Esq. was the first ; he was appointed by the request of Mrs. Derby herself, as well as on account of his peculiarly excellent qualifications as a teacher and estimable character as a man. He filled the office from 1791 to July 1805, when he resigned the situation. His successor was Rev. Andrews Norton, now Professor of Sacred Literature, in the University at Cambridge. He continued in the office but a short time. He was succeeded by Mr. James Day, who remained one year, when Mr. Samuel Merrill was appointed. In 1808, Rev. Daniel Kimball accepted the appointment of Preceptor and continued in the office until 1826, when Mr. Increase S. Smith, the present Preceptor was appointed.

The Preceptress is Miss Susan Waterman, and the Assistant Preceptress, Miss Elizabeth C. Norton.

The present number of scholars is 78 ; 33 males and 45 females.

The present Board of Trustees is composed of the following gentlemen, viz. :

Rev. John Allyn, D. D. of Duxbury,
" Peter Whitney, of Quincy,
" N. B. Whitney, of Hingham,
" Jacob Flint, of Cohasset,
Dr. Levi Lincoln, of Hingham,
Hon. James Savage, of Boston,
    Martin Lincoln, Esq. of Hingham,
Dr. Cushing Otis, of Scituate,
" Robert Thaxter, of Dorchester,
Rev. Charles Brooks, of Hingham,
    Ezra W. Sampson, Esq. of Braintree.

My information respecting the public schools,* is principally derived from the Chairman of the School Committee of 1826. The statement for this year, corresponds very nearly, with the existing facts, the arrangement of the schools, not having been materially altered for the present year. In 1826, the whole number of public schools was thirteen, five male and eight female. Three of the male schools are kept, each, during the whole year, and two of them for six months each; the female schools for six months each.

The number of youth in Hingham, between the ages of 4 and 16, is 879.

In 1827, October, the number of scholars on the lists of the eight female schools, was 334, and on the three summer male schools, 204.

In 1826, the amount of money paid for salaries to school teachers, was $1740.

The number of scholars attending private schools, was in 1826, 150, and the amount paid for private tuition, was $898.

---

* The earliest date, at which a public school was established in Hingham, cannot be ascertained. The earliest notice of the erection of a school house is found in the Selectmens' First Book of Records, which appears to have been in the year 1668. In 1670, Mr. Henry Smith contracted with the selectmen, "to teach and instruct, until the year be expired, in Latin, Greek and English, writing and arithmetic, such youths of the inhabitants of Hingham," as should be sent to their school. His salary was fixed at £24, to be paid quarterly, in wheat, rye, barley, peas and Indian corn, at current prices. In 1673, James Bates, Senior, was paid "for keeping school." In 1674, Joseph Andrews and James Bates received compensation as school masters. In 1677, James Bates made a written agreement with the selectmen to teach "Latin, English, writing and arithmetic," for one year for £20 sterling. In 1679, Matthew Hawke was paid by the town, for teaching a school. In 1685, Mr. Thomas Palmer contracted with the selectmen, to teach Latin, Greek, English, writing and arithmetic for £20; £10 in money, and £10 in corn. In 1687, Mr. Samuel Shepard was

The salary of the preceptor of the academy, is $700 per year, and that of the preceptress $300; the assistant preceptress receives $150 per year.

These expenditures are exclusive of those for books, fuel, rents, repairs, &c. &c. There is also one private seminary (Misses Cushings') for young ladies, the expenses of which are not embraced in this statement, the scholars who attend it being principally from other towns.

ECCLESIASTICAL HISTORY. The first church in Hingham, was formed in September, 1635, and is ranked by Mr. Savage (in his note on the early churches in Massachusetts, in Winthrop, vol. i. p. 95) as the twelfth that was formed in Massachusetts proper. Rev. Peter Ho-

employed as a teacher of Latin, &c. with a salary of £25 in corn. In 1690, Mr. Richard Henchman was a teacher. In 1694, Mr. Joseph Estabrook, Jr. contracted to teach Latin, Greek, &c. for £22 per year, one half to be paid in money, and the other in corn. Mr. Estabrook continued until 1696, when Mr. Jedidiah Andrews (afterwards a minister at Philadelphia) was employed for a salary of £30 in money. Mr. Estabrook was again employed in 1700, and continued until 1705, Aug. 20, when Mr, John Odlin was engaged; but he remained for only a short time. Mr. Joseph Marsh (the same probably, who was afterwards the minister of Quincy), was employed in 1706 and 1707. After him, Mr. Daniel Lewis, who subsequently settled in the ministry at Pembroke, taught the school for several years. This note is already too long, and I give merely the names of a few other teachers. 1712-13, Mr. Jonathan Cushing; 1713-14, Mr. Cushing and Mr. John Norton, Jr. From April, 1714, to 1717, Mr. Job Cushing, afterwards the minister of Shrewsbury. 1718, Mr. Allen, Mr. Cornelius Nye and Mr. Adam Cushing. Mr. Nye taught a school in the north part of the town, from 1718 to 1745, with the exception only of two or three years. Perhaps previously, and during that time, other schools were established in other parts of the town. The south part of the town and the east precinct drew their proportion of money from the treasury, and appropriated it for the support of schools as they thought proper. Mr. Isaac Lincoln, was a teacher of the school in the north part of the town for a long series of years. He died April 19, 1760, aged 59. From the foregoing list, it appears that well educated teachers were early employed in this town, to instruct the youth. They were generally men of liberal education.

bart of Hingham, England, with his family, arrived at
Charlestown in June, 1635, where his father's family had
arrived before him.* Several of his friends from Hingham, England, and others† had already settled in this
town. It is said (on the authority of Mather) that
he declined the invitations of several towns to become
their minister ; prefering to join the new settlement at
Bare Cove, (which on the second of September, 1635,
received the name of Hingham) and here he gathered the first church. Mr. Hobart and twenty-nine others drew for house lots on the 18th of Sept. 1635, but at
what time he actually settled here it is impossible, and
perhaps not material, to ascertain with perfect accuracy.
Nor can we discover from any record at what particular
time the first house of worship was erected. It was a
small building, surrounded with a palisadoe for the protection of the worshippers against any attack by the Indians. Its situation was very near the spot on which the
post office now stands, opposite the academy.

We have reason to suppose from the rapid increase of
the number of settlers in the course of the four or five
first years of the settlement of the town, that the church
soon became respectable in point of numbers and otherwise prosperous and flourishing. In the year 1638, Mr.

* "1633, Edmond Hobart, senior, came from Hingham, in Norfolk, (Eng.) with his wife, and his son Joshua, and his daughters
Rebecca and Sarah, and their servant Henery Gibbs, into New
England, and settled first at Charlestown, and after the said Edmond Hobart and his son Joshua and Henery Gibbs settled in this
town of Hingham."—*Manuscript of Daniel Cushing, 3d town
clerk of Hingham.*

† " 1633, Ralph Smith, Nicholas Jacob, and his cousin Thomas
Lincoln, (weaver), from Hingham, and Thomas Hobart, from
Windham, came from thence and settled in this Hingham.—*Cush-
ing's MSS.*

Robert Peck, a preacher of the gospel in Hingham, England, arrived in this country, and settled in Hingham.* He was ordained *teacher* of the church November 28th of that year. The people of Hingham were thus early blessed with the labours of two clergymen, the duty of one being to instruct the people in doctrine, and that of the other confined generally, to exhortation. But as remarked by Mather, "the good people of Hingham, did rejoice in this light (only) for a season." Mr. Peck, at the solicitation of his friends in England, returned to them in 1641,† and there remained a minister of the gospel. The first notice which can be found of the appointment of deacons, was in the year 1640. On the 29th of January of that year, Henry Smith and Ralph Woodward were chosen deacons, and they were ordained on the 2d of February following.‡

It does not appear that the harmony of the church or the prosperity of the town was interrupted until the year 1644, when the unfortunate occurrence of the military difficulties§ caused a serious injury to both. The prominent part which Mr. Hobart took in this unpleasant controversy, rendered him less popular at home, and obnoxious to the government. His friends, however, were much the most numerous and influential party in the church, and his conduct in relation to the minority, although it gave rise to some jealousy, and in a few instances to strong dislike, does not appear to have diminished the attachment which a majority of the citizens had uniformly exhibited towards him. From the severe and burthensome fines and expenses to which he was subjected in consequence

* Cushing's MSS.
† Hobart's Diary and Cushing's MSS.
‡ Hobart's Diary.
§ A full account of these difficulties may be found under the head of Civil History, in a subsequent part of this work.

of his zeal for popular rights, he appears to have been relieved by the liberality of the people of his charge.

His salary in 1648 was three score and ten pounds. It was the same for the two subsequent years. In 1651, the town voted that " Mr. Hobart should have five score pounds a year, for two years, for his maintenance and towards building of him a house." " Five score pounds" appears to have been his regular salary for many years afterwards.*

Nothing particularly worthy of mention occurred in the affairs of the church, until within about two months before the decease of Mr. Hobart, when his declining strength and inability to discharge the pastoral duties, rendered it necessary to ordain a successor. The person selected was Rev. John Norton. He was ordained pastor of the church Nov. 27, 1678. Mr. Hobart assisted in the services on the occasion. Mr. Norton was educated at Harvard University, where he graduated in 1671. He was a nephew to Mr. Norton, the Minister of Boston. The decease of the venerable Hobart took place January 20, 1678-9, in the 75th year of his age and 53d of his ministry; nine years of which he spent in Hingham, England. He was an indefatigable student, and his acquirements were various and extensive. " He was much admired (says Mather) for well studied sermons," and the remark is a just one, if we can judge from the manuscript copies of a few of them which are now preserved. Independent in his own feelings, vigour and strength were the characteristics of his discourses. They possess more of exhortation than of doctrine, and were calculated to produce the most salutary moral effects.†

---

* His salary was generally paid in rye, Indian corn, wheat, &c.
† A more particular account of Mr. Hobart's family may be found in a note at the end of the volume.

The successor of Mr. Hobart was of a more mild and conciliating spirit, with probably less extensive acquirements; but distinguished for his amiable character, fervent piety, and zeal for the promotion of true religion. He laboured in the ministry nearly thirty-eight years, and died on the third of October, 1716, in the 66th year of his age.

It was during the ministry of Mr. Norton, that the town voted to erect a new meeting-house; but as this subject produced considerable excitement, and as the proceedings in relation to it are blended in some measure with the civil history of the town, I have reserved an account of it for that department of this work.

After the decease of Mr. Norton, about twenty months elapsed before his successor was ordained. During that time candidates were heard, and on the 11th of February, 1716–17, the inhabitants concurred with the church, and "did then by a *major vote* carried in by papers with one hundred and five hands, chuse Mr. Samuel Fisk, of Braintree, to be the minister of said Hingham."* Mr. Fisk, it appears, did not accept this invitation of the inhabitants of Hingham to become their minister, and for what reason it is not known; perhaps, however, the vote in his favour might not have been unanimous, and this idea is supported by tradition.

On the 28th of March, 1717, the town voted to "grant unto a minister for a yearly salary one hundred and ten pounds in money, and a settlement of £200 to be paid in Province bills of credit, or in such money as usually passeth between man and man."

On the 9th of Sept. 1717, " The Church and Congregation voted and chose Mr. Thomas Prince to take the

*Town Records.

office of a pastor over the church of Christ and Congregation in Hingham."* Mr. Prince, also, declined the acceptance of this invitation. After Mr. Prince, Mr. EBENEZER GAY preached as a candidate, and on the 30th December, 1717, the church and congregation by their unanimous votes, gave him an invitation to become their pastor. Mr. Gay signified his acceptance of this harmonious call, which proved to be one of the most fortunate and happy events in the history of the church. He was ordained June 11, 1718.† The talents, learning, and liberal views of this eminent divine, were a rich blessing to the people of his charge, and have justly given him rank as "one of the greatest and most valuable men of his time."‡ He lived in the ministry for the remarkably long period of sixty-eight years, nine months, and a few days ; and died March 18, 1787, in the ninety-first year of his age.§ At his interment a discourse was delivered by Rev. Dr. Shute. An extract from that discourse, will show the opinions entertained of him, by an enlightened and liberal contemporary :

"But no encomium of mine (says Dr. Shute) can elevate your ideas of his amiable and excellent character, both as a christian, and as a minister of the gospel. You and your fathers, *are witnesses how holily and justly and unblamably he behaved himself;* and with what diligence and fidelity he discharged the duties of the ministerial office. Nor were his abilities, exerted in promoting the interest

* Town Records.
† "Mr. Belcher preached from 2d Tim. iv. 5, "*Make full proof of thy ministry.*" Mr. Danforth gave the Charge, Mr. Eells the Right Hand of Fellowship. With those Mr. Pickman and Mr. Niles laid on hands."—*Gay's Record.*
‡ This was the opinion expressed by Dr. Chauncy respecting Dr. Gay.
§ Dr. Gay was born at Dedham, Aug. 26, 1696.

of the Redeemer's kingdom, unknown to others ;—his light was so illustrious, that his praise is in all the churches. For learning—for liberality—candour, and strength of mind, he was distinguished and celebrated, by the judicious and candid. A particular and exact delineation of his character, however, is not pretended ; to draw which would require a pen equal to his own. True greatness needs no laboured panegyric.

But yet the pensive mind, habituated to esteem and veneration by a long uninterrupted course of friendship, will follow him beyond the grave, into the regions of immortality, and please itself in contemplating him as removed from all the imperfections incident to humanity, in this mortal state,—from the labours of mental pursuits,—from all doubts in points of speculation, *here* seen *through a glass darkly*,—from the debility and lassitude, which time, by the constitution of Heaven, produces in the human frame, and as *now* engaged in the service of his Maker, with unceasing ardour, and rejoicing before him, in the vigour of perpetual youth.

While we drop the friendly and sympathetick tear over the remains of your dear and venerable pastor, and contemplate his better part as having left this dark abode for the realms of eternal day ; we must wish to *die the death of the righteous, and that our last end may be like his.*"*

---

* The following obituary notice of Dr. Gay, was published March 30, 1787, and as every thing relating to this distinguished man is interesting, it is here inserted :—

" The Reverend Ebenezer Gay, D. D. Pastor of the First Church in Hingham, departed this life March 18th, 1787, in the 91st year of his age, and 69th of his ministry. To give a good man his deserved character, is not only justice to the dead, but charity to the living ; for while they *mark the perfect man, and behold the upright*, impressed with the amiableness of his virtues, they may be induced to imitate them, *and their end be peace*. This purpose, it is hoped, may be answered by a faint portrait of the Doctor's.

Dr. Gay retained his mental faculties in a remarkable degree of vigour to the very close of life. Of this, his justly celebrated sermon, entitled the *Old Man's Calendar*

"He had his education at Harvard College, he made distinguished proficiency in the knowledge of the classics, and various other sciences, and received his first degree in 1714. His inclination early led him to the study of divinity; and soon after he had received his second degree, he began to preach, and was ordained to the work of the ministry in Hingham, June 11, 1718. The duties of his office engrossed his whole attention; and making the Bible the rule of his faith he studied that sacred book with great diligence, and soon became mighty in the scriptures: in consequence of which he was led to a juster view of the plan of divine grace in the gospel, and to sentiments more liberal and candid, than were common in that day. His compositions were judicious—evidently the result of intense thought and application—calculated to give his hearers a knowledge of the method of reconciliation through the Mediator, and impress upon their minds a sense of moral obligation. The doctrines which he preached to others were enforced by his own example: his people are witnesses how holily, how justly, and unblamably he behaved himself among them. To them he readily afforded assistance in times of distress; and upon all occasions discovered, that their temporal as well as eternal interest lay near his heart. His heart and his doors were always open to his friends; and by his hospitality he secured the affectionate regard of all who visited his house.

"By his inoffensive and condescending conduct, he manifested the pacific disposition of his heart, and rendered his unwearied exertions to promote peace and good order more effectual. In ecclesiastical councils (to which he was formerly often invited) his wisdom and benevolence were conspicuous, and gave him great advantage in composing differences, and healing divisions subsisting in churches.

"Though his conversation abroad might seem reserved, yet in private, among his friends, it was free, instructive and edifying; the salutary effects of which have been sensibly felt by his brethren in the ministry; and his kind, parental treatment will ever be acknowledged by them. His prayers were rational and devout, and well adapted to the various occasions of life. Enthusiasm and superstition formed no part of his religious character. In his christian warfare, he did not entangle himself with the affairs of this life, but his conversation was in heaven. In times of sickness, and in the near views of dissolution, he appeared to have composure and resignation of mind, and hopes of full immortality.

which was delivered Aug. 26, 1781, from Joshua xiv. 10, is full evidence. This excellent production was re-printed in England, translated into the Dutch language and published in Holland, and several editions of it have been published in this country.*

"His prudent and obliging conduct rendered him amiable and beloved as a neighbour. His tender feelings for the distressed induced him to afford relief to the poor according to his ability. His beneficent actions indicated the practical sense he had of his Lord's own words—'It is more blessed to give than to receive.' The serenity of his mind, and evenness of his temper, under the infirmities of advanced years, made him agreeable to his friends, and continued to the last the happiness which had so long subsisted in his family; in which he always presided with great tenderness and dignity. A reflection on the indulgence of Heaven in the long enjoyment of so affectionate and worthy a parent, and the hopeful prospect of his happiness beyond the grave, must inspire them with gratitude, and lead them into a cordial acquiescence in the painful separation.

"The uncommon vigour of his mental powers, at that time of life, is evident from a printed sermon which he preached on the day when he completed the 85th year of his age. The University at Cambridge voluntarily conferred upon him the degree of Doctor of Divinity, in 1785, as an expression of their sense of his great merit.

"It was his greatest dread, he often said to his friends, to live beyond his usefulness: and it is remarkable, that by the continuance of his bodily and mental abilities, he was able to persevere in the ways of well-doing—to maintain the post assigned him, and go through all the duties of his office, to the very close of life.

"His death was sudden. On Lord's day morning he rose well as usual; while preparing for the pulpit, he was arrested by the harbinger of death, and, within an hour after, calmly resigned his useful life; and, like David of old, after he had served his generation, by the will of God fell on sleep.

"Through the long course of his ministry, he was greatly respected by his people: which is evident, not only by their attention to him while living, but by their kind offices at his interment.

"Thus lived and died that great and good man, the Reverend Doctor GAY, who now rests from his labours, and his works, we trust, follow him, in the ample rewards of grace and glory."— *Mass. Gazette.*

* Of the sermons of Dr. Gay which have been published, the following is a list, viz:—One delivered at the ordination of the Rev. Joseph Green of Barnstable, 1725; two lecture sermons in Hing-

It is worthy of remark that for the space of more than
a century and a half, the first parish was destitute of a
settled minister for only twenty months.

The number of baptisms recorded by Dr. Gay, during
his ministry, was 2801 ; the number of deaths (including
some belonging to Hingham who died in other places)
1349 ; and the number of couples married by him was 665.

The successor of Dr. Gay, and the fourth minister of
the first parish, was Rev. Henry Ware, D. D. of Sher-
burne, the present Hollis Professor of Divinity in Harvard University. He was educated at that University,
and graduated in 1785. He was ordained over the church
and congregation in Hingham Oct. 24, 1787.* In consequence of an invitation to the Professorship at Cambridge, Mr. Ware requested a dismission from the parish,
and the connexion was accordingly dissolved. Dr. Ware
delivered his valedictory discourse May 5, 1805. During
his ministry the number of persons baptized by him was
615, the number of marriages 185, and of deaths 489.

After the dissolution of Dr. Ware's connexion with the

---

ham, 1728 ; a sermon before the Ancient and Honourable Artillery
Company, 1728 ; a lecture in Hingham, on occasion of the arrival
of His Excellency J. Belcher, Esq. to this government, 1730 ; a sermon before several military companies in Hingham, 1738 ; a sermon delivered at Suffield at the ordination of Rev. Ebenezer Gay,
Jr. 1741–2 ; sermon at the funeral of Rev. J. Hancock, Braintree,
1744 ; an election sermon, 1745 ; sermon at the annual convention
in Boston, 1746 ; sermon in Boston at the ordination of Rev. J.
Mayhew, 1747 ; in Scituate, at the ordination of Rev. J. Dorby,
1751 ; in Keene, at the instalment of Rev. Ezra Carpenter, 1753 ;
in Yarmouth, at the instalment of Rev. Grindall Rawson, 1755 ;
Dudleian lecture, 1759 ; at the decease of Rev. Dr. Mayhew, in
Boston, 1766 ; in Hingham, at the ordination of Rev. Caleb Gan-
nett over a church in Nova Scotia, 1768 ; Thanksgiving Sermon,
Hingham, 1770 ; Old Man's Calendar, Hingham, 1781.

* The sermon on this occasion was delivered by Rev. T. Hilliard,
of Cambridge ; charge by Rev. J. Brown, of Cohasset ; and the right
hand of fellowship was presented by Rev. Mr. Shute of Hingham.

First Parish, several candidates were heard, and of those, Rev. Joseph Richardson, the present pastor, was preferred by a majority of the Parish. He accordingly received an invitation to settle here in the ministry. The invitation was accepted, and Mr. Richardson was ordained, July 2, 1806.* It is proper to mention that the members of the parish were not unanimous in extending this invitation to Mr. Richardson. The cause of this disaffection, and of the eventual separation of the opposers of the settlement of Mr. Richardson from the parish, and of their formation of a new society, are yet so fresh in the memory of most of those who will peruse these pages, that it is unnecessary for me to attempt to describe them, even if I had such an inclination. Besides, a detail of all the circumstances relating to this unpleasant controversy, would require too much space to be inserted in this work, and would answer no purpose, except as a record of my own opinion, which I certainly have no disposition to obtrude upon the public. The principal object of this history is to preserve *facts* and not *opinions* ; and I cannot persuade myself that it is incumbent on me, or desirable in any point of view, to describe the jealousies, the prejudices, or the unwise actions of the living, and especially those of which full accounts have been published to the world. If any one, however, has any relish for controversies of this description, or any disposition to refresh his memory with the accounts of this second " sad, unbrotherly contention" in Hingham, in which the clergy were involved, he may find all the details in two pamphlets published soon after its occurrence.

* The Sermon on this occasion was delivered by the late Dr. Bentley, of Salem ; the Charge by Rev. Mr. Barker, of Middleborough ; and the Right Hand of Fellowship was presented by Rev. Mr. Briggs, of Plympton.

To those who wish to read a *Vindication* of the proceedings of the First Parish, in the settlement of Mr. Richardson, I recommend a perusal of the letters of the late Dr. Bentley, of Salem, and of Rev. Mr. Norton, late of Weymouth, together with the other papers and statements published under the sanction of the names of the committees of the first church and parish. Those who are desirous of reading an opposite statement, will find the views of the opposers of Mr. Richardson's settlement, presented in a *Narrative* containing statements, letters, &c. with a reply to the vindication by a committee of the opposers; the whole collected and published by the late Dr. Thaxter.

I have thus given a sketch of the history of the First Church and Parish in Hingham, from 1635 to the present time, and in order to preserve the distinctness of the narration, I have omitted to notice the organization of the other churches during that period. There was, indeed, but one church in Hingham until the year 1721, when the Second Church was organized at Cohasset, or as it was then called Conohasset.*

Of the preliminary proceedings relating to the formation of the East Precinct, and of the subsequent establishment of a church at Conohasset, I shall now present a sketch, with some account of the clergy of the place.

In 1713, May 14, the proprietors of the undivided lands in Hingham gave their consent to the inhabitants of Conohasset, to erect a meeting house " on that land called the Plain."

At a town meeting held on the 7th day of March, 1714–15, the inhabitants of Conohasset " desired the town that they would be pleased to give their consent that they

---

* This name is sometimes written Conohasset, Conahasset, Conyhasset, and sometimes Konohasset, in our old records. " It signifies Fishing Promontory."—*Flint*. The town was incorporated by the name of Cohasset.

might be made a precinct, or that they might be allowed something out of the town treasury to help to maintain the worship of God amongst them, or that they might be abated that which they pay to the minister to maintain the worship of God at the *Town* : and the vote of the town passed in the *negative* concerning all the forementioned particulars."*

It is rather remarkable that a petition so reasonable should have been rejected. The inhabitants of Conohasset then presented their case to the General Court, but the inhabitants of Hingham persisted in opposing their petition and a committee was chosen "to give answer to it," at the General Court in June, 1715.

In July 1715, the town voted to remit to the inhabitants of Conohasset, their ministerial taxes, on the condition that they provide an *orthodox* minister among themselves, provided they *cheerfully* accept of the same." To this the inhabitants of Conohasset replied "that they could not cheerfully accept thereof."

In September following, the town voted to reimburse to the inhabitants of Conohasset, or to those that should afterwards inhabit in the first and second divisions of Conohasset uplands, and in the 2d part of the 3d division, all their ministerial and school taxes, so long as they should maintain an *orthodox* minister among themselves. This vote does not appear to have been satisfactory ; perhaps the condition was exceptionable. On the 12th of March, 1715–16, the town voted to remit to the inhabitants of Conohasset their ministerial and school taxes for that year, without any condition. This vote was not satisfactory. In November, 1716, a committee was chosen by the town to oppose the petition of the inhabitants of

---

* Town Records.

4*

Conohasset before the General Court, and again, in February 1716-17, an unsuccessful motion was made in town meeting, to agree with the inhabitants of Conohasset about a precinct.

In May, 1717, a committee was appointed by the town to meet the committee of the General Court, chosen to view the " lands and dwellings of the inhabitants of Conohasset, to see if it be convenient to make them a precinct." It was probably soon after this time, that the inhabitants of Conohasset obtained the privileges for which they had so long contended.*

Having erected their house of worship, and obtained the privileges of a parish, the inhabitants of Conohasset soon made arrangements for the settlement of a minister. Mr. Nehemiah Hobart, a grandson of Rev. Peter Hobart, the first minister of Hingham, preached to them as a candidate from July 13, 1721, to December 13th of that year, when he was ordained, the church having been organized on the day previous.† The character of Mr. Hobart may be concisely described in the words of Mr. Flint. " His character, which I early obtained from aged persons, who knew it, and from some of his writings which I have in my possession, appears to have been that of a tru-

---

* In the excellent century discourses of Rev. Jacob Flint, the present minister of Cohasset, it is stated that the inhabitants of Conohasset obtained the privilege of a parish in 1715, by a petition to General Court. This statement cannot be reconciled with the votes abovementioned, taken from the town records. This discrepancy of dates is not, however, very material.

† I give these statements on the authority of Rev. Nehemiah Hobart's journal, carefully copied by the late James O. Lincoln, Esq. whose perseverance and correctness in collecting information concerning the early history of this town cannot be too much commended. At the ordination of Mr. Hobart, Rev. Daniel Lewis of Pembroke delivered the sermon ; Rev. Mr. Pitcher of Scituate the charge, and Rev. Mr. Whitman of Hull gave the right hand of fellowship ; Rev. Mr. Gay of Hingham made the introductory prayer.

ly devout, enlightened and liberal divine. He had talents as a preacher, and virtues as a christian, which would have rendered him instructive and acceptable, in a learned and more numerous society. His worth was not much known abroad, but was justly and highly appreciated by his early instructer, neighbour, and constant friend, the excellent Gay." Mr. Hobart died May 31, 1740, in the 44th year of his age,* and in the 19th of his ministry. The first deacon of the church in Conohasset was John Jacob, the second Joseph Bates, and the third Lazarus Beal.†

After the decease of Mr. Hobart, several candidates were employed by the parish, and of those Mr. John Fowle of Charlestown was preferred.‡ He received an invitation to become the pastor of the church and society. This invitation was not extended to Mr. Fowle, by the unanimous consent of the parish. His opposers yielded however, to the wishes of the majority, and he was ordained Dec. 31, 1741.§ Mr. Fowle was a well educated and talented clergyman. He was graduated at Harvard University in 1732. He is said however to have possessed a very troublesome nervous temperament, "which rendered him unequal in his performances, and at times quite peevish and irregular." His physical infirmity rendered his opposers more numerous, and his pastoral relation was dissolved in the fifth year of his ministry.

At this period, the first house of worship was too small for the accommodation of the society, which had increased

* Mr. Hobart was born April 27, 1697.
† Hobart's Journal.
‡ Mr. Flint's century discourses, whence I have derived many of the subsequent statements relating to Conohasset.
§ At this ordination Rev. William Smith of Weymouth began with prayer; Rev. Hull Abbot of Charlestown delivered the sermon; Rev. Nathaniel Eells of Scituate gave the charge, and Rev. Ebenezer Gay of Hingham presented the right hand of fellowship.—*Mr. Fowle's Journal.*

in numbers and wealth. The erection of a new house was commenced near the time of Mr. Fowle's dismission, and it was completed in the course of the next year. This building was 60 feet in length and 45 in breadth. It was the same which is now standing. Before the completion of this house, several candidates were heard by the parish, and of those Mr. John Brown was preferred. He received an invitation to become their minister which was extended to him with great unanimity. He was ordained Sept. 2, 1747.*

Mr. Brown was a native of Haverhill. He received his education at Harvard University, where he was graduated in 1741. He was a man of genius, learning and wit. His sentiments were liberal, and his discourses indicated a correct taste and sound judgment. He was an active, zealous and efficient friend to the rights of his country; and by precept and example, he supported the principles which were maintained by the patriots of the American Revolution. He died in the 67th year of his age, and in the 45th of his ministry. It was during the ministry of Mr. Brown, that the east precinct in Hingham was set off and incorporated as a town by the name of Cohasset. I here leave the account of the ecclesiastical affairs of the place, having introduced so much of it as comes properly within the ecclesiastical history of Hingham.

The third church which was formed within the original limits of Hingham, was the same which is now styled the Second Church in Hingham, on account of the incorporation of Cohasset as a new town.† Of this church the first

---

* The services on this occasion were, introductory prayer by Rev. Wm. Smith of Weymouth; sermon by Rev. Ward Cotton; charge by Rev. Nathl. Eells; right hand of fellowship by Rev. Josiah Cotton; concluding prayer by Rev. Sheajashub Bourn of Scituate.

† The meeting-house of the second congregational parish was raised June 22, 1742. The Parish was set off March 25, 1745.

pastor was Rev. Daniel Shute, D. D. He was ordained Dec. 10, 1746. Dr. Shute was a native of Malden ; he was born July 19, 1722. He was educated at Harvard University and graduated in 1743. He was a truly eminent divine. He possessed a strong discriminating mind and great weight and respectability of character. His excellent acquaintance with human nature ; his literary acquirements, and the liberality of his political and religious sentiments, gave him great influence over the minds of men. His colloquial powers were fine, and his conversation always interesting and instructive. His discourses were sensible, practical and impressive. During the American Revolution, he advocated the cause of his country with zeal and earnestness. He was elected by his fellow citizens a member of the convention which formed the constitution of Massachusetts, and of that which adopted the constitution of the United States.*

He laboured in the ministry for a great length of time, but on account of a failure in his sight, he quitted his public labours in March, 1799 ; from which time he retained his pastoral relation until his decease, but voluntarily relinquished his salary. Rev. Nicholas Bowes Whitney, the present pastor of the church and society, was ordained his colleague Jan. 1, 1800.† Dr. Shute died Aug. 30, 1802, in the 81st year of his age and in the 56th of his ministry.‡

* His remarks in the latter convention, on the subject of a religious test, are worthy of a perusal : they may be found in a volume of debates on the federal constitution.
† At Mr. Whitney's ordination the sermon was delivered by Rev. Phineas Whitney of Shirley ; the charge by Rev. David Barnes, D. D. of Scituate, and the right hand of fellowship was presented by Rev. Mr. Ware, then pastor of the first church in Hingham.
‡ The following is an extract from a well written obituary notice of Dr. Shute, which appeared in the public papers a few days after his decease.

I have already spoken of the circumstances which gave rise to the formation of the present Third Congregational Church and Society in Hingham. This Society was incorporated by an Act of the Legislature, February 27, 1807 ; the church was organized, and assumed the name of the Third Church in Hingham, June 16, 1807. On the succeeding day, their present meeting house was dedicated to the worship of God, and their first minister,

"By the great strength of mind and clearness of perception, with which the God of Nature had distinguished him, cultivated by study and improved by accurate scholarship, he became eminent in his profession for public performances, which combined good sense, sound judgment, and extent of thought, with perspicuity of style, and a correct taste.

A firm believer in the Gospel, he had talents to give it an able support ; and the same clearness of intellect, liberality of mind, and patience of investigation, which gave him a rational view of its doctrines and principles, enabled him also to explain them with clearness, and inculcate them with success. Nor was it only by his public labours he endeavoured to promote the cause of religion ; he gave it also the support of an exemplary life. Liberal but not loose in his sentiments, he was equally displeased with that austerity, which covers religion with a perpetual gloom, and with that licentiousness, which strips her of her fairest ornaments. His religious opinions he formed with deliberation and adopted with caution ; but when once adopted, they were not lightly abandoned. He adhered to them tenaciously, and maintained them with firmness, till further light, to which his mind was always open, produced a different conviction.

In social life, though he suffered himself on no occasion to lose sight of his character as a clergymen, his natural cheerfulness and happy talent for pleasant and instructive conversation endeared him to his friends, and rendered him a pleasing guest to all who enjoyed his acquaintance ; for he knew how to support the decorum of a Christian Minister, and at the same time to display the affability and ease of an agreeable companion. He possessed, in a degree that few possess it, the talent of accommodating himself to persons of every age and description ; so that his society was always acceptable to the aged by his seriousness and gravity, to the learned by his talents, information and good sense, and to the young by the cheerfulness and pleasantry, with which he never failed to season conversation, and convey useful instruction."

Of the productions of his pen, there have been published an artillery election sermon, 1767 ; an election sermon, 1768 ; and a sermon on the death of Dr. Gay, 1787.

Rev. Henry Colman, was ordained.* Mr. Colman was educated at Dartmouth College. He continued the pastor of the Church and Society until 1820. His pastoral relation was dissolved, March 14th of that year, at his request, and by the consent of the society.

Rev. Charles Brooks, the present minister of the Third Society, succeeded Mr. Colman in the pastoral office. He was ordained January 17, 1821.† I have thus given a sketch of the history of the congregational societies in this town, to the time of the settlement of their present ministers; with their present state, the inhabitants are sufficiently acquainted, without the aid of any further description.

Of the nine ministers, who have been settled over the three congregational societies in Hingham, four only are dead, viz.: Messrs. Hobart, Norton, Gay and Shute. The aggregate number of years, which the four spent in the ministry, in this place, exceeds two centuries; averaging over fifty years to each. It may be remarked of them, that their talents, learning, and long continued and faithful services, have had the most favourable effects on the welfare of the town. They preserved for a long series of years, the utmost harmony in the churches, unanimity among the people, and a steady and liberal support to the institutions of religion.

There is also at the present time, a remarkable degree of unanimity in the religious opinions of the people. The ministers of the three societies do not differ in their

* On this occasion Rev. Henry Ware, D. D. delivered the sermon; Rev. Dr. Lathrop of Boston the charge; and Rev. Mr. Whitney of Hingham gave the right hand of fellowship.

† At the ordination of Mr. Brooks, the sermon was delivered by Rev. Dr. Ware of Cambridge; the charge by Rev. Dr. Harris of Dorchester; and the right hand of fellowship was presented by Rev. Mr. Francis of Watertown.

religious views, and are of the denomination called Unitarians. There are, however, some of other denominations in the town. An Universalist society has recently been formed, but they have no stated preacher. There are some Baptists, and a few Episcopalians; the former have stated, and the latter occasional preaching. There are also some of the Methodist persuasion.

CIVIL HISTORY. Previously to giving an account of the civil history of the town, I thought that some information respecting the origin, names and families of the first settlers, might be acceptable to most readers, although to some, the few pages which I devote to this purpose, will appear dry and uninteresting. The unfortunate loss of the town's first "great book of records," deprives me of one source of information, concerning the early proceedings of the town, in relation to civil affairs; but the preservation of the "smaller book of records," (imperfect as it is for many years,) the records of grants of land, the diary of the first minister, and the private papers of Daniel Cushing, Esq. to which I have before referred, enable me to present a pretty full account of the individuals who were the first settlers of Hingham. The original name of the place was Bare, or Bear Cove.* The exact date at which any individual came here to reside, cannot be ascertained. Among the papers of Mr. Cushing, there is a "list of the names of such persons as came out of the town of Hingham, and towns adjacent, in the county of Norfolk, in the Kingdom of England, into New England and settled in Hingham." From this list, we are led to believe there were inhabitants here as early as

* "Perhaps (says the editor of Winthrop) it sometimes was thought a natural resort of bears; perhaps, sometimes the appearance of the cove at low water, regulated the letters used to express the same sound."

1633, and among them Ralph Smith, Nicholas Jacob with his family, Thomas Lincoln, weaver, Edmund Hobart and his wife, from Hingham, and Thomas Hobart with his family, from Windham,* in Norfolk, England.— During the same year, Theophilus Cushing, Edmund Hobart, senior, Joshua Hobart, and Henry Gibbs, all of Hingham, England, came to this country. Cushing lived some years at Mr. Haines's farm, and subsequently removed to Hingham.† The others settled at Charlestown, and in 1635 removed to this place. In 1634, there were other settlers here, and among them Thomas Chubbuck; Bare Cove was assessed in that year.‡ In 1635, at the May court, Joseph Andrews was sworn as constable of the place. There was a considerable increase of the number of settlers, and in that year grants of lands were made to upwards of fifty individuals, of which a record is preserved. It was in June of that year that Rev. Peter Hobart arrived at Charlestown,§ and soon after, settled in this place.

I here subjoin the names of those who settled or received grants of land here, in the respective years mentioned. Possibly there may be some names omitted, which have escaped my observation, and those of others inserted to whom lands were granted, but who never settled here. The list is as perfect, however, as long, careful and patient examination of public and private records can make it. The names of those of whose families

* Now called Wymondham.
† Theophilus Cushing died here in March, 1678–9, aged about 100 years.
‡ The assessment was as follows: Boston, Dorchester and Newton each £80; Roxbury £70; Watertown £60; Sagus and Ipswich each £50; Salem and Charlestown each £45; Medford £26; Wessaguscus £10; Bare Cove £4.
§ See page 22.

there are lineal descendants, or collateral branches in Hingham, at the present time, are distinguished by small capitals ; and the names of those who removed to other places are in italics ; those whose names are extinct here, or of whom there are no descendants in this town, are in the common letter.

In 1635, in addition to those before mentioned, (viz. : JOSEPH ANDREWS,* Thomas Chubbuck, Henry Gibbs, EDMUND HOBART,† sen., EDMUND HOBART, Jr., JOSHUA HOBART, Rev. PETER HOBART, THOMAS HOBART, NICHOLAS JACOB, THOMAS LINCOLN, weaver, Ralph Smith,) were *Jonas Austin*,‡ *Nicholas Baker*,§ CLEMENT BATES, Richard Betscome, Benjamin Bozworth, William Buckland, *James Cade*,‖ Anthony Cooper, John Cutler,¶ John Farrow, Daniel Fop, JARVICE GOULD, WM. HERSEY,** Nicholas

* The first town clerk of Hingham.
† It may be remarked that this name has been written differently; generally, however, either Hobart or Hubbard. Mr. Hobart the first minister usually wrote it Hobart, although the record of his father's death is, "father Hubbard died."
‡ The name of Jonas Austin afterwards appears in Taunton.
§ Nicholas Baker twice a delegate from Hingham to the General Court, afterwards removed to Scituate, where he was settled as pastor of the church. Mather speaks of him as "honest Nicholas Baker ; who, though he had but a private education, yet being a pious and zealous man, or, as Dr. Arrowsmith expresses it, so good a logician that he could offer up to God a reasonable service ; so good an arithmetician that he could wisely number his days ; and so good an orator that he persuaded himself to be a good christian ; and, being also one of good natural parts, especially of a strong memory, was chosen pastor of the church there ; and in the pastoral charge of that church he continued about eighteen years." He died August 22, 1678.
‖ James Cade's name appears in Yarmouth in 1640.
¶ Cushing's MSS. date his arrival in 1637. He had a grant of land in 1635.
** This name is written in various ways ; often in our early records Hersie ; sometimes Harsie : frequently Hearsey ; but of late years Hersey. It is, I believe, a name of French origin. Among the surnames of the noblemen and gentlemen who went over to England with William the Conqueror, was that of Hersy.

Hodsdin, Thos. Johnson,* ANDREW LANE, Wm. Large,†
THOMAS LORING, George Ludkin,‡ Jeremy Morse, William Nolton, JOHN OTIS§, David Phippeny, John Palmer, John Porter, Henry Rust, John Smart, Francis Smith, (or Smyth,‖) John Strong¶, Henry Tuttil,** William Walton,†† THOMAS ANDREWS, William Arnall, George Bacon, Nathaniel Baker, Thomas Collier, GEORGE LANE, GEORGE MARSH, Abraham Martin,‡‡ Nathaniel Peck, Richard Osborn, Thomas Wakely, THOMAS GILL, Richard Ibrook, William Cockerum,§§ William Cockerill, JOHN FEARING,‖‖ John Tucker.

* A person by the name of Johnson formerly kept a tavern in a building situated on the spot where the dwelling-house of Mr. Benjamin S. Williams now stands. It was known by the name of the Pine Tree Tavern, from the circumstance that a very large pine tree stood in its front. This family removed to Stoughton.
† William Large removed to Provincetown, C. C.
‡ George Ludkin died at Braintree, February 20, 1648.
§ John Otis, the common ancestor of the distinguished civilians, patriots and orators of that name in this country. There are branches of his family in Scituate, Barnstable, Boston and in other places. This name in our old records is written variously: Otis, Oates, Otties, and Oattis.
‖ Francis Smith removed to Taunton.
¶ John Strong removed to Taunton, from thence to Northampton. He was probably the ancestor of the families of that name in that town and vicinity.
** Tuttil, according to Cushing's MSS. came over in 1637. His grants of land were in 1635.
†† Walton's Cove derives its name from a person of this name.
‡‡ Martin's Well, or as it was sometimes called, Abraham's Well, derives its name from this person.
§§ Cockerum probably returned to England. "October 3, 1642, brother Cockram sailed for England."—*Hobart's Diary.*
‖‖ John Fearing came from Cambridge, England. The arrival of a person by this name is dated in Cushing's MSS., 1638. It may be observed that in a few instances, according to Cushing's MSS., the persons to whom grants of land were made did not arrive here until after the date of their grants. This may have been the fact, but there were evidently many more settlers here before 1640 than are mentioned in these manuscripts. He mentions but four families that came over in 1635. Unquestionably a much larger number accom-

In 1636, JOHN BEAL,* senior, Anthony Eames,† THOMAS HAMMOND, Joseph Hull,‡ RICHARD JONES, Nicholas Lobdin, Richard Langer, JOHN LEAVITT,§ *Thomas Lincoln, Jr.*, miller,|| THOMAS LINCOLN, cooper,|| Adam Mott,

panied Mr. Hobart. It is possible, however, that the trifling discrepancies in the dates of the arrival of some of the settlers may be reconciled by the supposition that there were in some instances two or more persons of the same name; indeed, we know that four persons of the same christian and surname, (Thomas Lincoln) came into this town within a few years after its first settlement.

* " 1638, John Beale, shoemaker, with his wife and five sons and three daughters and two servants, came from Old Hingham and settled in New Hingham."—*Cushing's MSS.*

† Anthony Eames was a deputy in 1637, 1638 and 1643; frequently a town officer, and involved in the military difficulties in 1644, 1645, &c.

‡ Joseph Hull, a deputy from Hingham in September, 1638, and in March after. One of the commissioners to end small causes, in the same year.

§ The family tradition concerning John Leavitt is, that he was an indented apprentice in England, and that he absconded from his master and came to this country when nineteen years of age, and settled first at Roxbury and afterwards in Hingham. If this tradition is correct he must have arrived in this country before the year 1628, as he died November 20, 1691, aged 83. He received a grant of land in this town in 1636. His homestead was in Leavitt-street, (recently so named) on both sides of the river, and is now principally owned by the descendants of his sons Israel and Josiah. He was a deacon of the church. In his will, executed November 30, 1689, and proved January 27, 1691-2, he mentions his sons Samuel, Israel, Moses, Josiah, Nehemiah, and the widow of his son John; also, his daughters Mary, Sarah, Hannah and Abigail. Israel had a son John; he died July 29, 1749. John, son of this John, died April 13, 1797, aged 86. The late Mr. Jacob Leavitt was a son of this last mentioned John; he died January 7, 1826; he possessed good natural abilities and a sound judgment; he was a valuable citizen; he filled many public offices, and was a zealous whig of the revolution. Mr. Joshua Leavitt who died May 12, 1825, aged 92, and who filled the office of town treasurer for thirty years with so much acceptance, was a descendant of Josiah Leavitt, son of the first John above mentioned.

|| For an account of the Lincolns, see note in a subsequent part of this work.

Thomas Minard, John Parker, George Russell, WILLIAM SPRAGUE,* George Strange, Thomas Underwood, Samuel Ward, Ralph Woodward,† John Winchester, William Walker.

In 1637, THOMAS BARNES, Josiah Cobbit, *Thomas Chaffe*,‡ *Thomas Clapp*,§ William Carlslye, (or Carsly,) *Thomas Dimock*,|| Vinton Dreuce, Thomas Hett, Thomas Joshlin, Aaron Ludkin, John Morrick, THOMAS NICHOLS, Thomas Paynter, Edmund Pitts,¶ Joseph Phippeny, Thomas Shave, Ralph Smith, Thomas Turner, JOHN TOWER, Joseph Underwood, William Ludkin,** *Jonathan Bozworth*.††

In 1638, there was a considerable increase of the number of settlers. Among them were, Mr. *Robert Peck*, (see page 23,) *Joseph Peck*‡‡, *Edward Gilman*,§§ John Foul-

---

* William Sprague, with his brothers Richard and Ralph, arrived at Naumkeag (Salem,) in 1628 or 29; from thence they removed to Mishawum (Charlestown,) and from thence William removed to Hingham; his house lot was on the south side of Pleasant-street. He had several sons; among them, Anthony, William and John. This William removed to Rhode Island. Anthony the eldest son had a numerous family; he lived and died in a house situated near that in which Mr. Samuel Gilbert now resides, at the place called "Over the River." Josiah Sprague was one of Anthony's sons; Isaac was one of Josiah's six sons; he purchased the place now owned by Joshua Sprague, his grandson, on which stands one of the oldest dwelling-houses in Hingham.

† Ralph Woodward, one of the first deacons of the church—see 23d page.

‡ Thomas Chaffe removed to Swanzey.

§ Thomas Clapp removed to Scituate.

|| Thomas Dimock removed to Barnstable.

¶ Edmund Pitts, according to Cushing's MSS., came over in 1639, with his brother, Leonard Pitts and Adam Foulsham. His grant of land was in 1637.

** William Ludkin was from Norwich, England.

†† Jonathan Bozworth removed to Swanzey.

‡‡ Mr. Joseph Peck removed to Rehoboth, where he died, Dec. 22, 1663.

§§ Edward Gilman removed to New Hampshire.

sham, Henry Chamberlin, Stephen Gates, George Knights, *Thomas Cooper*,* MATTHEW CUSHING,† JOHN BEAL, Jr., Francis James, Philip James, James Buck, *Stephen Payne*,‡ William Pitts, Edward Michell, *John Sulton*,§ STEPHEN LINCOLN.‖

Samuel Parker, THOMAS LINCOLN,¶ Jeremiah Moore, *Mr. Henry Smith*,** *Bozoan Allen*,†† MATTHEW HAWKE,‡‡ WILLIAM RIPLEY.§§ All of those preceding, who came to

* Thomas Cooper removed to Rehoboth.

† A memorandum of a descendant of Matthew Cushing mentions the date of his arrival at Boston, August 10, 1638. The name of his wife was Nazareth Pitcher. Their children, whose names follow, came with them to this country, viz. : Daniel, Jeremiah, Matthew, Deborah, and John. Matthew Cushing, senior, died September 30, 1660, aged about 72 years. He was probably the ancestor of all of the name in this country. His son John removed to Scituate, where he was a selectman in 1676, a deputy, and afterwards, about the year 1690, an assistant. His son and grandson were judges of the Supreme Court of this State, and the latter, (Hon. William Cushing,) of the Supreme Court of the United States.

‡ Stephen Payne removed to Rehoboth, where he died in 1677.

§ One of the same name removed to Rehoboth. He came from Attleborough, England. One of the same name was among the first inhabitants of Conohasset, perhaps a son of the eldest John.

‖ See note on the Lincoln families, in the last part of this work.

¶ Thomas Lincoln, the husbandman.

** Mr. Henry Smith's name appears afterwards in Rehoboth.

†† Bozoan Allen, "the very good friend" of Mr. Hobart, the first minister, came from Lynn, England. He was often a deputy, a military officer and an influential citizen of Hingham. He was very active in the military difficulties in 1644, 1645, &c. He removed to Boston, where he died September 14, 1652.

‡‡ Matthew Hawke was the second town clerk of Hingham. He was from Cambridge, England.

§§ In a brief genealogy of the family of William Ripley, collected by one of his descendants, it is stated, that he "accompanied Mr. Hobart in the new settlement." If by this it is meant that he came to this country with Mr. Hobart, or that he was here before 1638, I am inclined to believe the statement is erroneous. The grant of land to William Ripley is in 1638, and in the list of settlers prepared by Mr. Cushing, there is the following memorandum : "1638, William Ripley and his wife and two sons and two daughters, came from Old Hingham and settled in New Hingham." His this country in 1638, took passage in the ship Diligent of Ipswich, John Martin, master.* In addition to these the following named persons received grants of land in the year 1638, viz: John Buck, John Benson, THOMAS JONES,† Thomas Lawrence, John Stephens, JOHN STODDER,‡ Widow MARTHA WILDER,§ THOMAS THAXTER.‖

In 1639, Anthony Hilliard and John Prince received

name is by him embraced, as above stated, in the list of those who took passage in the ship Diligent of Ipswich. He was admitted a freeman, May 18, 1642. He died in July, 1656. His two sons were John and Abraham. John married a daughter of Rev. Peter Hobart. John had six sons, viz.: John, Joshua, Jeremiah, Josiah, Peter, and Hezekiah. Of these, John and Peter died in this town. Joshua removed to Haddam, Connecticut. Jeremiah to Kingston, Massachusetts. Josiah to Weymouth. Hezekiah died in Connecticut in 1691. Peter had three sons, Peter, Nehemiah, and Ezra. Nehemiah removed to Plymouth. Peter remained in Hingham. He had two sons, Noah and Nehemiah. Noah removed to Barre. Nehemiah remained in Hingham. His wife was a daughter of Rev. Nehemiah Hobart, of Cohasset. Mr. Nehemiah Ripley, now living, is one of his sons.

* Cushing's MSS.

† This name is frequently written Joanes in the old records.

‡ This name is sometimes written as above, and frequently Stoddard.

§ For an account of the Wilder family, see note at the end of the volume.

‖ Thomas Thaxter, the common ancestor of all of the name in this town and vicinity. The name of his wife was Elizabeth. He died in 1654, his wife surviving him. His sons who lived to manhood were John and Samuel. John had twelve children. He died March, 1686-7. His widow was married to Daniel Cushing, Esq. Three of the daughters of John, married Cushings. One of his sons was Col. Samuel Thaxter, a magistrate, delegate to the General Court, an assistant and otherwise distinguished in public trusts. He had four children, Elizabeth, John, Samuel, and Sarah. Elizabeth was married to Capt. John Norton, son of Rev. John Norton, and afterwards to Col. Benjamin Lincoln, father of the late Gen. Lincoln of the revolutionary army. Samuel H. U. 1714, married Sarah Marshall of Boston, and after her decease, Mary Hawke, daughter of James Hawke. She survived him and was afterwards married to Rev. John Hancock of Braintree, father of Hon. John Hancock, president of the Continental Congress. Maj. Samuel Thaxter, the son of Samuel and Sarah H. U. 1743, was one of the very few who grants of land. The name of Hewett (Huet*) and Liford, are mentioned in Hobart's Diary, in that year, and in the Diary the following names are first found in the respective years mentioned : in 1646, BURR,† in 1647, JAMES WHITON ; in 1649, JOHN LAZELL, SAMUEL STOWELL ; in 1653, GARNETT‡ and CANTERBURY.§

The number of persons who came over in the ship Diligent, of Ipswich, in the year 1638, and settled in escaped the massacre at Fort William Henry. Maj. Thaxter had a numerous family, among whom were the late Dr. Thomas Thaxter, Dr. Gridley Thaxter, of Abington, (still living,) Samuel, &c. The late Capt. Duncan M. B. Thaxter was a son of Samuel. John, the eldest son of Col. Samuel Thaxter, married Grace Stockbridge, of Pembroke. His son, Col. John Thaxter, H. U. 1741, was a delegate in 1772. John Thaxter, Esq. of Haverhill was a son of Col. John Thaxter. Dea. Joseph Thaxter was a brother of Col. John Thaxter, and father of the late Rev. Joseph Thaxter, minister of Edgartown, and a Chaplain of the army of the Revolution.

David Thaxter was the only son of the eldest Samuel who lived to manhood. He married Alice Chubbuck. He had but one son, David, who died in 1791, aged 83. Several of his children are yet living.

* The following singular account of the cure of one of this name, of a distempered imagination is extracted from the History of New England. Mass. His. Col. New Series, vol. 6, p. 442.

" 1642. One Huet's wife, of Hingham, having been long in a sad, melancholy distemper, near to frenzy, and having formerly, in the year 1637, attempted to drown her child, did now again take her child of three years old, and stripping it of its clothes, threw it into the creek, but it scrambling out of the water and mud, came to the mother, who took it another time and threw it so far into the creek that it could not possibly get out ; yet by good providence, a young man that accidentally passed by took it up. The mother conceived she had sinned the sin against the Holy Ghost. She was afterwards proceeded with by church council, and by that means was brought off from those satanic delusions ; and after the manifestations of repentance, was received into the church again, being brought to a sound mind."

† Simon Burr, the first of the name of Burr in this town, came from Dorchester, and was related to Rev. Jonathan Burr an early minister in that town.

* Garnett now written Gardner.

† Canterbury extinct as a surname. The Barnes families are descendants from Cornelius Canterbury.

Hingham, was 133. All that came before were 42, making in all 175. The whole number that came out of Norfolk (chiefly from Hingham, and its vicinity) from 1633 to 1639, and settled in this Hingham, was 206.* This statement on the authority of the third town clerk of Hingham, must be reconciled with the fact, that there was a much larger number of settlers here in 1639, than would appear from his estimate. They undoubtedly came in from other places, and I am inclined to believe that there may be some omissions in Mr. Cushing's list. It may be remarked here, that many of the names mentioned in the previous pages are now scattered in various parts of the country. Many of the first settlers removed to other places during the militia difficulties which occurred within a few years after the settlement of the town; and a considerable number had previously obtained lands at Rehoboth.†

The earliest record to be found of the proceedings of the town in relation to the disposition of the lands, is in 1635. In June of that year grants were made to a considerable number of individuals, and on the 18th of September as has been before stated, thirty of the inhabitants drew for house lots, and received grants of other lands for the purposes of pasture, tillage, &c.

* Cushing's MSS.

† Among the towns of which a considerable number of inhabitants originated in Hingham, are Rehoboth, Wareham, Cummington, Dennysville and Perry, (Maine.) A few removed to Swanzey, Duxbury, Scituate, Barnstable, Lancaster, &c. &c. and a large number to Boston.

The following names appear in Lancaster in 1654, viz: Stephen Gates, senior, James Whiting or Witton, John Towers and Thomas Joslin. Persons of the same names had previously received grants of land in Hingham, and actually settled here. The Pecks of Rehoboth, Fearings of Wareham, Clapps and Otises of Scituate, Dimocks and Otises of Barnstable, Lincolns of Taunton, New Bedford, Dennysville and Perry, (Me.) &c. &c. originated here.

It was in July, 1635, that a plantation was erected here,* and on the 2d of September following that, the town was incorporated by the name of Hingham,† from which it appears that there are but eleven towns in this State and but one in the county of Plymouth, older than Hingham. I cannot ascertain satisfactorily when the first meeting for civil purposes was held. It is stated by Mr. Flint in his century discourses, to have been on the 18th of September, 1635. There is as much evidence in our town records and in those of Cushing's MSS. which I have examined, that the first town meeting was held in June of that year, as in September. The statements in the same discourses, that the inhabitants of Hingham arrived in 1635, and that they obtained deeds of land from the natives to form the town previously to holding the first town meeting, are unquestionably erroneous, being at variance with our town records, Cushing's MSS. and the Indian deed itself.‡

The house lots drawn on the 18th of September, 1635, were situated on the "*Town street,*" the same which is now called North street. During that year the settlement was extended to "*Broad Cove street,*" recently named Lincoln Street. In the year following, house lots were granted in the street now called South street and in the northerly part of "*Bachelor street,*" now Main street.§

* "By this establishment or erection of a plantation, we must not understand that settlements were then first made at the spot, but that a municipal government was permitted there, or that the place was allowed to have deputies in the General Court."—*Winthrop's Journal, v.* 1, *p.* 163 ; *note by Mr. Savage.*
† So named on account of the origin of the pastor and most of the people from the town of that name in Norfolk, England.
‡ Daniel Cushing was the third town clerk of Hingham, and not the second as supposed by Mr. Flint.
§ "September 18th, 1635.—It is agreed upon that every man

Some idea of the relative wealth of several towns in 1635, may be estimated from the following apportionment of the public rate for that year. Newton and Dorchester were assessed each £26 5; Boston £25 10; Salem £16; Hingham £6; Weymouth £4; &c. In 1637, the number of men furnished by this town to make up the number of 160 to prosecute the war against the Pequods, was 6; Boston furnished 26, Salem 18, Weymouth 5, Medford 3, Marblehead 3. The assessment upon this town at the General Court in August following, was £8 10; the least, except that of Weymouth, which was £6 16. Property and population appear to have been unequally distributed and often fluctuating. In 1637, we find the first record of the choice of a town clerk. Joseph Andrews was chosen, and in 1638, the first record of the choice of assessors.*

that is admitted to be a townsman, and has lots granted him, shall bear charges both to Church and Commonwealth, proportionably to his ability; and in case he shall sell his lots, he shall first tender them to the town, and in case the town shall refuse to give what it shall be worth, or find a chapman to buy them, then it shall be lawful for him to sell them, always provided that it be an *honest man* that shall be placed into the said lots."—*Town Records.*

* They were Edmund Hobart, Anthony Eames, Thomas Hammond, Nicholas Jacob, Henry Rust, Joseph Andrews.

The following curious order passed to enforce attendance at public meetings:

"14th May, 1637.—It is likewise agreed upon by a joint consent and general vote of the freemen, that whosoever shall absent himself from any meeting appointed and shall have lawful warning of it, or shall otherwise come to the knowledge of the same meeting without special occasion approved of by the assembly or the major part of the freemen then assembled; and further, it is likewise agreed upon that when assembled and be come together to agitate and determine of any business concerning the common good of Church or Commonwealth, not one shall depart until the assembly be broken up or without leave, upon the payment of every such defect, *one peck of Indian corn*, as well for the not staying with the assembly being there assembled as for the not coming, having lawful warning or otherwise [having] knowledge of it. And likewise it is agreed upon, that every such fine or fines shall be levied by the

From the year 1638 until 1641, the imperfect records of the town contain nothing of particular interest. On the 9th of April of the latter year, the town passed an order fixing the wages of labourers and the prices of commodities.* In 1643, June 12, Anthony Eames, Samuel Ward and Bozoan Allen had leave from the town to set up a corn mill near the cove, on the condition that they paid any damage caused by flowage, &c.† This mill was undoubtedly erected before the year 1645, as we find recorded in November of that year, that Gowan Wilson was removed by the town from the office of miller.

constable, and shall be carefully kept to the use of the town as hereafter shall be thought fit to employ it, and from the day of the date hereof it shall stand in force, unless it be found to be prejudicial and repealed.

* The following is a copy of the order referred to : "It is ordered and agreed upon by a joint consent, that the prices of labourer's wages and commodities within this town should be affixed as follows: Upon every commodity as well as upon labourer's wages should be abated *three* pence upon the *shilling* of what has been formerly taken.

	s.	d.
Common labourers a day	1	6
For mowing a day	2	0
Carpenters a day	1	10
A team with 3 yoke of oxen and one man, a day	7	00
with 2 yoke, a mare and a man	7	00
2 yoke and one man	6	00
1 yoke, a mare and a man	5	4

and they are to work eight hours a day.

Taylors and shoemakers are to abate three pence on the shilling of what they took before for a day's work.——Butter the lb. 5d.

Wheelwrights are to abate three pence on the shilling and to charge 2 shillings a day."

In 1641 the following persons were chosen to make a rate, viz : Thomas Cop, Edward Gilman, John Oatis, John Porter, Bozoan Allen, and Joseph Andrews.

† In a note to Winthrop's Journal, vol. ii. p. 294, it is stated that Thomas Joy, a carpenter, (who was employed to obtain subscribers to Dr. Child's celebrated petition to government) removed from Boston to Hingham, where "he built and owned the town mill." His removal to Hingham was probably in 1646. It would seem that the mill was built before his removal to Hingham ; yet being a car-

It appears, that at an early date, there was a controversy respecting a portion of the lands embraced within the limits of Nantasket, or Nantascot. The inhabitants of Hingham claimed, and endeavoured to maintain a title to them, as in July, 1643, we find the following record, viz. : " There is chosen by the town, Joseph Peck, Bozoan Allen, Anthony Eames, and Joshua Hubbard, to go to the next court to make the best improvement of the evidence the town have for the property of Nantascot, and to answer the suit that now depends, &c."

In the records of the General Court, (vol. ii. p. 35,) there is recorded the following peremptory decision on this subject, in September, 1643. " The former grant to Nantascot was again voted and confirmed, and Hingham were willed to forbear troubling the Court any more about Nantascot."

penter he might have been employed to build it. On a loose paper among the manuscripts of Daniel Cushing, I find a sketch of a conveyance of a mill with a recital as follows : " Whereas Thomas Joy, heretofore of the town of Boston, and late inhabitant of the town of Hingham, &c. carpenter, deceased, did in his life time some years before his death make a feoffment of a grist mill standing in the town cove at Hingham aforesaid, with some houses, lands and meadows lying, &c. (which he the said Joy purchased of Bozone Allen,) to his father-in-law John Gallop of Boston, seaman, &c. &c." This evidence led me to suppose the impression of the author of the note in Winthrop to be erroneous, viz : "that Joy *built* and owned the town mill." My supposition was that the first mill was built by those who had liberty from the town, and that it was originally owned by them and sold to Joy. In answer to some inquiries made to the author of the note referred to, relating to the evidence of the fact that Joy built the first mill, I have been furnished with the following statement and extracts from the Registry of Deeds for Suffolk County. Although relating merely to a corn mill, they may be amusing to some readers. He writes as follows :—" In Vol. ii. of our Registry of deeds p. 77 Thos. Joy, of Boston, carpenter, conveys to Richard Church of Charlestown, carpenter, " the one half or moiety of all that corn mill standing and being at Hingham in New England, and half the foundation of a saw mill adjoining to

Previously to the difficulties of 1644, we have reason to suppose that the town was flourishing and prosperous. The situation was eligible—the facilities for fishing, and for intercourse with other towns by water, contributed to enrich it. In 1654, it is described by Johnson, in his Wonder Working Providence, in the following manner, viz. : "A place nothing inferiour to their Neighbours for scituation, and the people have much profited themselves by transporting Timber, Planke and Mast for shipping to the town of Boston, as also ceder and Pine-board to supply the wants of other townes, and also to remote parts, even as far as Barbadoes. They want not for fish for themselves and others also. This towne consisted of about sixty families, the forme is somewhat intricate to describe, by reason of the Seas wasting crookes where it beats upon a mouldering shore, yet have they compleat it, with half the dam, wharf-head and stream whereon the said mills do stand, called the town's cove, with one half or moiety of the lot of land lying thereunto, containing four or six acres of land, be it more or less, which formerly were the lands of Abraham Martyn," &c. &c. this was 4 February 1653. It appears in a later page of the same volume, p. 83 that previously, scil. 24 January 1653 Joy had leased by indenture to Church for 21 years the same moiety. After the record of the indenture is this curious memorandum. "It is agreed betwixt the said parties, that they shall as soon as the corn mill is finished to grind, they shall within six days next after set upon the framing and finishing the saw mill." Next follows, " A testimony, in reference to the present covenant, Nathaniel Sowther, aged about 62 years, deposeth and saith, that about the 24 January 1653 this deponent engrossed a pair of indentures made betwixt Thomas Joy and Richard Church for the moiety of the mill at Hingham with other things for the term of one and twenty years, but the said term was not to begin until the mill and dam was finished that she might be able to grind corn, and therefore there was a blank left to put in the date and to commence from the day that the said mill was set on work and grind corn, notwithstanding the said indentures were sealed and acknowledged before the Governor with mutual consent to put in the date after the mill was set on work. Taken upon oath this 19 of Octor. 1654." The indenture is recorded *with the blank.*"

streetes in some places. The people joyned in Church covenant in this place, were much about an hundred soules, but have been lessened by a sad unbrotherly contention, which fell out among them wasting them every way, continued already for seven yeares space, to the great grief of all other Churches," &c. It is this " sad, unbrotherly contention" which first attracts our attention in the early history of Hingham. It is to be regretted, that most of the contemporary writers of the time when these difficulties arose, should have been of that class which disapproved of the proceedings of a majority of the citizens of the town, and that no statement by those opposed to them in opinion, has been preserved ; because by comparing opposite statements we should perhaps view the conduct of our ancestors, (then considered unjustifiable and disorderly,) as the result of principles more consonant to the spirit of the present age, than to the feelings of men at the time when they lived.

I am aware, however, that there is justice in the remark of the learned editor of Winthrop, when speaking of Governor Winthrop's account of these affairs, he says, " an unusual fairness for a party whose feelings had been so much engaged in the controversy is here shown by our author." These difficulties originated among the members of the military company, gradually enlisted the feelings of the whole town, arrested the attention of the church, were taken cognizance of by the neighbouring churches, and at last required the interposition of the government. A sketch of the rise, progress and termination of these difficulties may not be uninteresting ; illustrating, as it will, the principles of our fathers, and giving some indication of the spirit and asperity of controversies, when the prejudices of religion and of politics were unfortunately blended together. Winthrop, in his journal, vol. ii. p. 221, introduces the subject as follows:

"1645. This court fell out a troublesome business which took up much time. The town of Hingham, having one Emes their lieutenant seven or eight years, had lately chosen him to be their captain, and had presented him to the standing council for allowance ; but before it was accomplished the greater part of the town took some light occasion of offence against him, and chose one Allen to be their captain, and presented him to the magistrates (in the time of the last general court) to be allowed. But the magistrates, considering the injury that would hereby accrue to Emes, (who had been their chief commander so many years, and had deserved well in his place, and that Allen had no other skill, but what he learned from Emes,) refused to allow of Allen, but willed both sides to return home, and every officer to keep his place, until the court should take further order. Upon their return home, the messsengers, who came for Allen, called a private meeting of those of their own party, and told them truly what answer they received from the magistrates, and soon after they appointed a training day, (without their lieutenant's knowledge,) and being assembled, the lieutenant hearing of it came to them, and would have exercised them as he was wont to do, but those of the other party refused to follow him, except he would show them some order for it. He told them of the magistrates' order about it : the others replied that authority had advised him to go home and lay down his place honourably. Another asked, what the magistrates had to do with them ? Another, that it was but three or four of the magistrates, and if they had been all there, it had been nothing, for Mr. Allen had brought more for them from the deputies, than the lieutenant had from the magistrates. Another of them professeth he will die at the sword's point, if he might not have the choice of his own officers. Another (viz. the clerk of the band) stands up above the people, and requires them to vote, whether they would bear them out in what was past and what was to come. This being assented unto, and the tumult continuing, one of the officers (he who had told them that authority had advised the lieutenant to go home and lay down his place) required Allen to take the captain's place; but he not then accepting it, they put it to vote, whether he should be their captain. The vote passing for it, he then told the company, it was now past question, and thereupon Allen accepted it, and exercised the company two or three days, only about a third part of them followed the lieutenant. He, having denied in the open field, that authority had advised him to lay down his place, and putting (in some sort) the lie upon those who had so reported, was the next Lord's day called to answer it before the church, and he standing to maintain what he had said, five witnesses were produced to convince him. Some of them affirmed the words, the others explained their meaning to be, that one magistrate had so advised him. He denied both. Whereupon the pastor, one Mr. Hubbert, (brother to three of the principal in this sedition,) was very forward to have excommunicated the lieutenant presently, but, upon some opposition, it was put off to the next day. Thereupon the lieutenant and some three or four more of the chief men of the town informed four of the next magistrates of these proceedings, who forthwith met at Boston about it, (viz. the deputy governour, the serjeant major general, the secretary, and Mr. Hibbins.) These, considering the case, sent warrant to the constable to attach some of the principal offenders (viz. three of the Hubbards and two more) to appear before them at Boston, to find sureties for their appearance at the next court &c. Upon the day they came to Boston, but their said brother the minister came before them, and fell to expostulate with the said magistrates about the said cause, complaining against the complainants, as talebearers &c. taking it very disdainfully that his brethren should be sent for by a constable, with other high speeches, which were so provoking, as some of the magistrates told him, that, were it not for respect to his ministry, they would commit him. When his brethren and the rest were come in, the matters of the information were laid to their charge, which they denied for the most part. So they were bound over (each for other) to the next court of assistants. After this five others were sent for by summons (these were only for speaking untruths of the magistrates in the church.) They came before the deputy governour, when he was alone, and demanded the cause of their sending for, and to know their accusers. The deputy told them so much of the cause as he could remember, and referred them to the secretary for a copy, and for their accusers he told them they knew both the men and the matter, neither was a judge bound to let a criminal offender know his accusers before the day of trial, but only in his own discretion, least the accuser might be taken off or perverted &c. Being required to give bond for their appearance &c. they refused. The deputy laboured to let them see their errour, and gave them time to consider of it. About fourteen days after, seeing two of them in the court, (which was kept by those four magistrates for smaller causes,) the deputy required them again to enter bond for their appearance &c. and upon their second refusal committed them in that open court.

"The general court falling out before the court of assistants, the Hubberts and the two which were committed, and others of Hingham, about ninety, (whereof Mr. Hubbert their minister was the first,) presented a petition to the general court, to this effect, that whereas some of them had been bound over, and others committed by some of the magistrates for words spoken concerning the power of the general court, and their liberties, and the liberties of the church &c. they craved that the court would hear the cause &c. This was first presented to the deputies, who sent it to the magistrates desiring their concurrence with them, that the cause might be heard &c. The magistrates, marvelling that they would grant such a petition, without desiring conference first with themselves, whom it so much concerned, returned answer, that they were willing the cause should be heard, so as the petitioners would name the magistrates whom they intended, and the matters they would lay to their charge &c. Upon this the deputies demanded of the petitioners' agents (who were then deputies of the court) to have satisfaction in those points, whereupon they singled out the deputy governor, and two of the petitioners undertook the prosecution. Then the petition was returned again to the magistrates for their consent &c. who being desirous that the deputies might take notice, how prejudicial to authority and the honour of the court it would be to call a magistrate to answer criminally in a cause, wherein nothing of that nature could be laid to his charge, and that without any private examination preceding, did intimate so much to the deputies, (though not directly, yet plainly enough,) showing them that nothing criminal &c. was laid to his charge, and that the things objected were the act of the court &c. yet if they would needs have a hearing, they would join in it. And indeed it was the desire of the deputy, (knowing well how much himself and the other magistrates did suffer in the cause, through the slanderous reports wherewith the deputies and the country about had been possessed,) that the cause might receive a public hearing.

"The day appointed being come, the court assembled in the meeting house at Boston. Diverse of the elders were present, and a great assembly of people. The deputy governour, coming in with the rest of the magistrates, placed himself beneath within the bar, and so sate uncovered. Some question was in court about his being in that place (for many both of the court and the assembly were grieved at it.) But the deputy telling them, that, being criminally accused, he might not sit as a judge in that cause, and if he were upon the bench, it would be a great disadvantage to him, for he could not take that liberty to plead the cause, which he ought to be allowed at the bar, upon this the court was satisfied.

"The petitioners having declared their grievances &c. the deputy craved leave to make answer, which was to this effect, viz. that he accounted it no disgrace, but rather an honour put upon him, to be singled out from his brethren in the defence of one so just (as he hoped to make that appear) and of so public concernment. And although he might have pleaded to the petition, and so have demurred in law, upon three points, 1, in that there is nothing laid to his charge, that is either criminal or unjust; 2, if he had been mistaken either in the law or in the state of the case, yet whether it were such as a judge is to be called in question for as a delinquent, where it doth not appear to be wickedness or wilfulness; for in England many erroneous judgments are reversed, and errours in proceedings rectified, and yet the judges not called in question about them; 3, in that being thus singled out from three other magistrates, and to answer by himself for some things, which were the act of a court, he is deprived of the just means of his defence, for many things may be justified as done by four, which are not warrantable if done by one alone, and the records of a court are a full justification of any act, while such record stands in force. But he was willing to waive this plea, and to make answer to the particular charges, to the end that the truth of the case, and of all proceedings thereupon might appear to all men.

"Hereupon the court proceeded to examine the whole cause. The deputy justified all the particulars laid to his charge, as that upon credible information of such a mutinous practice, and open disturbance of the peace, and slighting of authority, the offenders were sent for, the principal by warrant to the constable to bring them, and others by summons, and that some were bound over to the next court of assistants, and others that refused to be bound were committed; and all this according to the equity of laws here established, and the custom and laws of England, and our constant practice here these fifteen years. And for some speeches he was charged with as spoken to the delinquents, when they came before him at his house, when none were present with him but themselves, first, he appealed to the judgment of the court, whether delinquents may be received as competent witnesses against a magistrate in such a case; then, for the words themselves, some he justified, some he explained so as no advantage could be taken of them, as that he should say, that the magistrates could try some criminal causes without a jury, that he knew no law of God or man which required a judge to make known to the party his accusers (or rather witnesses) before the cause came to hearing. But two of them charged him to have said, that it was against the law of God and man so to do, which had been absurd, for the deputy professed he knew no law against it, only a judge may sometimes, in discretion, conceal their names &c. least they should be tampered with, or conveyed out of the way &c.

"Two of the magistrates and many of the deputies were of opinion that the magistrates exercised too much power, and that the people's liberty was thereby in danger; and other of the deputies (being about half) and all the rest of the magistrates were of a different judgment, and that authority was overmuch slighted, which, if not timely remedied would endanger the commonwealth, and bring us to a mere democracy. By occasion of this difference, there was not so orderly carriage at the hearing, as was meet, each side striving unseasonably to enforce the evidence, and declaring their judgments thereupon, which should have been reserved to a more private debate, (as after it was,) so as the best part of two days was spent in this public agitation and examination of witnesses &c. This being ended, a committee was chosen of magistrates and deputies, who stated the case, as it appeared upon the whole pleading and evidence, though it cost much time and with great difficulty did the committee come to accord upon it.

"The case being stated and agreed, the magistrates and deputies considered it apart, first the deputies having spent a whole day, and not attaining to any issue, sent up to the magistrates to have their thoughts about it, who taking it into consideration, (the deputy always withdrawing when that matter came into debate,) agreed upon these four points chiefly; 1. that the petition was false and scandalous, 2. that those who were bound over &c.

and others that were parties to the disturbance at Hingham, were all offenders, though in different degrees, 3. that they and the petitioners were to be censured, 4. that the deputy governour ought to be acquit and righted &c. This being sent down to the deputies, they spent divers days about it, and made two or three returns to the magistrates, and though they found the petition false and scandalous, and so voted it, yet they would not agree to any censure. The magistrates, on the other side, were resolved for censure, and for the deputy's full acquittal. The deputies being thus hard held to it, and growing weary of the court, for it began [3] 14, and brake not up (save one week) till [5] 5, were content they should pay the charges of the court. After, they were drawn to consent to some small fines, but in this they would have drawn in lieutenant Emes to have been fined deeply, he being neither plaintiff nor defendant, but an informer only, and had made good all the points of his information, and no offence found in him, other than that which was after adjudged worthy of admonition only ; and they would have imposed the charges of the court upon the whole trained band at Hingham, when it was apparent, that divers were innocent, and had no hand in any of these proceedings. The magistrates not consenting to so manifest injustice, they sent to the deputies to desire them to join with them in calling in the help of the elders, (for they were now assembled at Cambridge from all parts of the United Colonies, and diverse of them were present when the cause was publickly heard, and declared themselves much grieved to see that the deputy governour should be called forth to answer as a delinquent in such a case as this was, and one of them in the name of the rest, had written to him to that effect, fearing least he should apprehend over deeply of the injury &c.), but the deputies would by no means consent thereto, for they knew that many of the elders understood the cause, and were more careful to uphold the honour and power of the magistrates than themselves were liked of, and many of them (at the request of the elder and others of the church of Hingham during this court) had been at Hingham, to see if they could settle peace in the church there, and found the elder and others the petitioners in great fault &c. After this (upon motion of the deputies) it was agreed to refer the cause to arbitrators, according to an order of court, when the magistrates and deputies cannot agree &c. The magistrates named six of the elders of the next towns, and left it to them to choose any three or four of them, and required them to name six others. The deputies finding themselves now at the wall, and not daring to trust the elders with the cause, they sent to desire that six of themselves might come and confer with the magistrates, which being granted, they came, and at last came to this agreement, viz. the chief petitioners and the rest of the offenders were severally fined, (all their fines not amounting to 50 pounds,) the rest of the petitioners to bear equal share to 50 pounds more towards the charges of the court, (two of the principal offenders were the deputies of the town, Joshua Hubbert and Bozone Allen, the first was fined 20 pounds, and the other 5 pounds,) lieutenant Emes to be under admonition, the deputy governour to be legally and publicly acquit of all that was laid to his charge.

"According to this agreement, [5] 3, presently after the lecture the magistrates and deputies took their places in the meeting house, and the people being come together, and the deputy governour placing himself within the bar, as at the time of hearing &c. the governour read the sentence of the court, without speaking any more, for the deputies had (by importunity) obtained a promise of silence from the magistrates. Then was the deputy governour desired by the court to go up and take his place again upon the bench, which he did accordingly, and the court being about to arise, he desired leave for a little speech, which was to this effect.

"I suppose something may be expected from me, upon this charge that is befallen me, which moves me to speak now to you ; yet I intend not to intermeddle in the proceedings of the court, or with any of the persons concerned therein. Only I bless God, that I see an issue of this troublesome business. I also acknowledge the justice of the court, and, for mine own part, I am well satisfied, I was publickly charged, and I am publickly and legally acquitted, which is all I did expect or desire. And though this be sufficient for my justification before men, yet not so before the God, who hath seen so much amiss in my dispensations (and even in this affair) as calls me to be humble. For to be publickly and criminally charged in this court, is matter of humiliation, (and I desire to make a right use of it,) notwithstanding I be thus acquitted. If her father had spit in her face, (saith the Lord concerning Miriam,) should she not have been ashamed seven days ? Shame had lien upon her, whatever the occasion had been. I am unwilling to stay you from your urgent affairs, yet give me leave (upon this special occasion) to speak a little more to this assembly. It may be of some good use, to inform and rectify the judgments of some of the people, and may prevent such distempers as have arisen amongst us. The great questions that have troubled the country, are about the authority of the magistrates and the liberty of the people. It is yourselves who have called us to this office, and being called by you, we have our authority from God, in way of an ordinance, such as hath the image of God eminently stamped upon it, the contempt and violation whereof hath been vindicated with examples of divine vengeance. I entreat you to consider, that when you choose magistrates, you take them from among yourselves, men subject to like passions as you are. Therefore when you see infirmities in us, you should reflect upon your own, and that would make you bear the more with us, and not be severe censurers of the failings of your magistrates, when you have continual experience of the like infirmities in yourselves and others. We account him a good servant, who breaks not his covenant. The covenant between you and us is the oath you have taken of us, which is to this purpose, that we shall govern you and judge your causes by the rules of God's laws and our own, according to our best skill. When you agree with a workman to build you a ship or house &c. he undertakes as well for his skill as for his faithfulness, for it is his profession, and you pay him for both. But when you call one to be a magistrate, he doth not profess nor undertake to have sufficient skill for that office, nor can you furnish him with gifts &c. therefore you must run the hazard of his skill and ability. But if he fail in faithfulness, which by his oath he is bound unto, that he must answer for. If it fall out that the case be clear to common apprehension, and the rule clear also, if he transgress here, the errour is not in the skill, but in the evil of the will : it must be required of him. But if the cause be doubtful, or the rule doubtful, to men of such understanding and parts as your magistrates are, if your magistrates should err here, yourselves must bear it.

"For the other point concerning liberty, I observe a great mistake in the country about that. There is a two fold liberty, natural (I mean as our nature is now corrupt) and civil or federal. The first is common to man with beasts and other creatures. By this, man, as he stands in relation to man simply, hath liberty to do what he lists; it is a liberty to evil as well as to good. This liberty is incompatible and inconsistent with authority, and cannot endure the least restraint of the most just authority. The exercise and maintaining of this liberty makes men grow more evil, and in time to be worse than brute beasts: omnes sumus licentia deteriores. This is that great enemy of truth and peace, that wild beast which all the ordinances of God are bent against, to restrain and subdue it. The other kind of liberty I call civil or federal, it may also be termed moral, in reference to the covenant between God and man, in the moral law, and the politic covenants and constitutions, amongst men themselves. This liberty is the proper end and object of authority, and cannot subsist without it; and it is a liberty to that only which is good, just and honest. This liberty you are to stand for, with the hazard (not only of your goods, but) of your lives, if need be. Whatsoever crosseth this is not authority, but a distemper thereof. This liberty is maintained and exercised in a way of subjection to authority; it is of the same kind of liberty wherewith Christ hath made us free. The woman's own choice makes such a man her husband; yet being so chosen, he is her lord, and she is to be subject to him, yet in a way of liberty, not of bondage; and a true wife accounts her subjection her honour and freedom, and would not think her condition safe and free, but in her subjection to her husband's authority. Such is the liberty of the church under the authority of Christ, her king and husband; his yoke is so easy and sweet to her as a bride's ornaments; and if through frowardness or wantonness &c. she shake it off, at any time, she is at no rest in her spirit, until she take it up again; and whether her lord smiles upon her, and embraceth her in his arms, or whether he frowns, or rebukes, or smites her, she apprehends the sweetness of his love in all, and is refreshed, supported and instructed by every such dispensation of his authority over her. On the other side, ye know who they are that complain of this yoke and say, let us break their bands &c. we will not have this man to rule over us. Even so, brethren, it will be between you and your magistrates. If you stand for your natural corrupt liberties, and will do what is good in your own eyes, you will not endure the least weight of authority, but will murmur, and oppose, and be always striving to shake off that yoke; but if you will be satisfied to enjoy such civil and lawful liberties, such as Christ allows you, then will you quietly and cheerfully submit unto that authority which is set over you, in all the administrations of it, for your good. Wherein, if we fail at any time, we hope we shall be willing (by God's assistance) to hearken to good advice from any of you, or in any other way of God; so shall your liberties be preserved, in upholding the honour and power of authority amongst you."

The following notes of the proceedings of the deputies and magistrates in relation to this affair, were collected by Mr. Savage, and published in his edition of Winthrop.

"The *first* order of the magistrates is, as follows: Fined the persons after named at such sums as hereafter are expressed, having been as moderate and gone as low as they any ways could with the holding up of authority in any measure, and the maintenance of justice, desiring the concurrence of the deputies herein, that at length an end may be put to this long and tedious business.

Joshua Hubbard is fined	£20,00,00
Edmond Hubbard,	5,00,00
Thomas Hubbard,	2,00,00
Edmond Gold,	1,00,00
John Faulshame,	20,00,00
John Towers,	5,00,00
Daniel Cushin,	2,10,00
William Hersey,	10,00,00
Mr. Bozon Allen,	10,00,00
Mr. Peter Hubbard, that first subscribed the petition	2,00,00

All the rest of the petitioners, being 81, out of which number are excepted three, viz. Mr. Peter Hubbard, John Foulshame and John Towres, the rest making 78, are fined 20 shillings a piece, the sum of which is 155,10,00

"We have also voted, that according to the order of the general court, for so long time as their cause hath been in handling, the petitioners shall bear the charge of the general court, the sum of which costs is to be cast up and agreed by the court, when the cause is finished.

"The house of deputies having issued the Hingham business before the judgment of our honoured magistrates upon the case came down, they have hereunder expressed their determinate censures upon such as they find delinquent in the case, viz.

Joshua Hubbard is fined	£20,00,00
Anthony Eames,	5,00,00
Thomas Hubbard,	4,00,00
Edmond Hubbard,	10,00,00

Daniel Cushan,	4,00,00
William Hersey,	4,00,00
Mr. Allen, beside his proportion with the train band,	1,00,00
Edmond Gold,	2,00,00
Total,	£50,00,00

"The rest of the train band of Hingham, that have an equal vote allowed them by law for the choice of their military officers, are fined 55 pounds to be paid by equal proportion, the which said sums of 50 and 55 pounds are laid upon the said delinquents for the satisfying of the charge of the court occasioned by the hearing of the cause, in case the said charge shall arise to the sum of 105 pounds. The deputies desire the consent of the magistrates herein.

"Several discordant votes passed each branch before the business was brought to its close."

After giving an account of the proceedings of the court, Winthrop remarks as follows :

"I should have mentioned in the Hingham case, what care and pains many of the elders had taken to reconcile the differences which were grown in that church. Mr. Hubbert, the pastor there, being of a Presbyterial spirit, did manage all affairs without the church's advice, which divers of the congregation not liking of, they were divided in two parts. Lieutenant Emes &c. having complained to the magistrates, as is before expressed, Mr. Hubbert, &c. would have cast him out of the church, pretending that he had told a lie, whereupon they procured the elders to write to the church, and so did some of the magistrates also, whereupon they stayed proceeding against the lieutenant for a day or two.

But he and some twelve more of them, perceiving he was resolved to proceed, and finding no way of reconciliation, they withdrew from the church, and openly declared it in the congregation. This course the elders did not approve of. But being present in the court, when their petition against the deputy governour was heard, Mr Hubbert, perceiving the cause was like to go against him and his party, desired the elders to go to Hingham to mediate a reconciliation (which he would never hearken to before, being earnestly sought by the other party, and offered by the elders) in the interim of the court's adjournment for one week. They readily accepted the motion, and went to Hingham, and spent two or three days there, and found the pastor and his party in great fault, but could not bring him to any acknowledgment. In their return by water, they were kept twenty four hours in the boat and were in great danger by occasion of a tempest which arose in the night ; but the Lord preserved them."

But the difficulties did not terminate here. The authority of government was resisted when the marshal attempted to levy the fines imposed on the petitioners. The following is Winthrop's account of the matter :

"1646. 26. (1.)] The governour and council met at Boston to take order about a rescue which they were informed of to have been committed at Hingham upon the marshal, when he went to levy the fines imposed upon Mr. Hubberd their pastor and many others who joined with him in the petition against the magistrates &c. and having taken the information of the marshal and others, they sent out summons for their appearance at another day, at which time Mr. Hubberd came not, nor sent any excuses, though it was proved that he was at home, and that the summons was left at his house. Whereupon he was sent for by attachment directed to the constable, who brought him at the day of the return. And being then charged with joining in the said rescue by animating the offenders, and discouraging the officer, questioning the authority of his warrant because it was not in the king's name, and standing upon his allegiance to the crown of England, and exemption from such laws as were not agreeable to the laws of England, saying to the marshal that he could never know wherefore he was fined, except it were for petitioning, and if they were so waspish that they might not be petitioned, he knew not what to say to it &c. All the answer he would give was, that if he had broken any wholesome law not repugnant to the laws of England, he was ready to submit to censure. So he was bound over to the next court of assistants.

"The court being at Boston, Mr. Hubberd appeared, and the marshal's information and other concurrent testimony being read to him, and his answer demanded, he desired to know in what state he stood, and what offence he should be charged with, or what wholesome law of the land, not repugnant to the law of England, he had broken. The court told him, that the matters he was charged with amounted to a seditious practice and derogation and contempt of authority. He still pressed to know what law &c. He was told that the oath which he had taken was a law to him ; and beside the law of God which we were to judge by in case of a defect of an express law. He said that the law of God admitted various interpretations &c. Then he desired to see his accusers. Upon that the marshal was called, who justified his information. Then he desired to be tried by a jury, and to have the witnesses produced viva voce. The secretary told him that two were present, and the third was sworn to his examination, (but in that he was mistaken, for he had not been sworn,) but to satisfy him, he was sent for and sworn in court. The matters testified against him were his speeches to the marshal before thirty persons, against our authority and government &c. 1. That we were but as a corporation in England ; 2. That by our patent (as he understood it) we could not put any man to death, nor do divers other things which we did ; 3. That he knew not wherefore the general court had fined them, except it were for petitioning, and if they were so waspish (or captious) as they might not be petitioned &c. and other speeches tending to disparage our authority and proceedings. Accordingly a bill was drawn up &c. and the jury found that he seemed to be ill affected to this government, and that his speeches tended to sedition and contempt of authority. Whereupon the whole court (except Mr. Bellingham, who judged him to deserve no censure, and desired in open court to have his dissent recorded) adjudged him to pay 20 pounds fine, and to be bound to his good behaviour, till the next court of assistants, and then farther if the court should see cause. At this sentence his spirit rose, and he would know what the good behaviour was, and desired the names of the jury, and a copy of all the proceedings, which was granted him, and so he was dismissed at present."

In 1646, the celebrated petition of Dr. Child and six others, for the abolition of " the distinctions which were maintained here, both in civil and church estate," and that the people of this country might be wholly governed by the laws of England, was presented to the house of deputies. Six of the petitioners were cited before the court and charged with great offences contained in this petition: they appealed to the parliament of England, and offered security to abide by their sentence; but the court thought proper to sentence the offenders to fine and imprisonment. The petitioners then resolved to lay their case before parliament, and Dr. Child, Mr. Vassall, and Mr. Fowle went to England for that purpose,* but it appears that they met with very ill success in their exertions. Their papers were published at London, by Major John Child, brother of Dr. Robert Child, in a tract, entitled *New England's Jonas cast up at London*, in allusion, probably, to the remark of Mr. Cotton, in one of his sermons, "that if any shall carry any writings or complaints against the people of God, in this country to England, it would be as *Jonas in the ship*." This tract was answered by Mr. Winslow, who was then in England, in another tract, entitled the *Salamander*, " wherein (says Winthrop) he cleared the justice of the proceedings" of the government here.

I introduced this notice of the petition of Dr. Child and others, for the purpose of correcting an errour into which Hutchinson and Neal have fallen, in confounding this controversy with that of our military dispute, which created so much excitement in the country. It is proper to mention, however, that Mr. Hobart was suspected of "having a hand in it," and consequently was obliged to suffer another of the mortifications to which the relentless spirit of persecution had subjected him. I give, however, Winthrop's account of his treatment in his own words.

* An amusing account of the superstitious terror of some of the passengers in the vessel in which the petitioners went to England, and of the ill success of their petition, may be found in Neal's History of New England.

"In 1646. (9.) 4.] This court the business of Gorton &c. and of the petitioners, Dr. Child &c. were taken into consideration, and it was thought needful to send some able man into England, with commission and instructions, to satisfy the commissioners for plantations about those complaints; and because it was a matter of so great and general concernment, such of the elders as could be had were sent for, to have their advice in the matter. Mr. Hubbard of Hingham came with the rest, but the court being informed that he had an hand in a petition, which Mr. Vassall carried into England against the country in general, the governour propounded, that if any elder present had any such hand &c. he would withdraw himself. Mr. Hubbard sitting still a good space, and no man speaking, one of the deputies informed the court, that Mr. Hubbard was the man suspected, whereupon he arose, and said, that he knew nothing of any such petition. The governour replied, that seeing he was now named, he must needs deliver his mind about him, which was, that although they had no proof present about the matter of the petition, and therefore his denial was a sufficient clearing &c. yet in regard he had so much opposed authority, and offered such contempt to it, as for which he had been lately bound to his good behaviour, he thought he would (in discretion) withdraw himself &c. whereupon he went out. Then the governour put the court in mind of a great miscarriage, in that our secretest counsels were presently known abroad, which could not be but by some among ourselves, and desired them to look at it as a matter of great unfaithfulness, and that our present consultations might be kept in the breast of the court, and not be divulged abroad, as others had been."

Winthrop then remarks upon a special providence of
God, (as he terms it,) in which he takes it for granted,
that Mr. Hobart, the people of Hingham and Dr. Child
entertained similar views, if they did not openly combine
their efforts to promote them.

"I must here observe a special providence of God,
pointing out his displeasure against some profane persons, who took part with Dr. Child &c. against the government and churches here. The court had appointed a
general fast, to seek God (as for some other occcasions,
so) in the trouble which threatened us by the petitioners
&c. The pastor of Hingham and others of his church
(being of their party) made light of it, and some said
they would not fast against Dr. Child and against themselves; and there were two of them (one Pitt and Johnson) who, having a great raft of masts and planks
(worth forty or fifty pounds) to tow to Boston, would
needs set forth about noon the day before (it being impossible they could get to Boston before the fast;) but
when they came at Castle Island, there arose such a tempest, as carried away their raft, and forced them to cut
their masts to save their lives. Some of their masts and
plank they recovered after, where it had been cast on
shore; but when they came with it to the Castle, they
were forced back again, and were so oft put back with
contrary winds &c. as it was above a month before they
could bring all the remainder to Boston."

The editor of Winthrop in noticing these remarks very
justly observes " that unless we be careful always to consider the cause of any special providence, we may fail in
our views of the displeasure of God;" and notices the
fact that the clergy when they came to this town, to reduce the church members to sobriety " were kept twenty

four hours in the boat, and were in great danger by occasion of a tempest."

The last time at which Mr. Hobart was made to feel the displeasure of the government, was in 1647. Winthrop mentions it in the following manner:

"4. (6). There was a great marriage to be solemnized at Boston. The bridegroom being of Hingham, Mr. Hubbard's church, he was procured to preach, and came to Boston to that end. But the magistrates, hearing of it, sent to him to forbear. The reasons were, 1. for that his spirit had been discovered to be averse to our ecclesiastical and civil government, and he was a bold man, and would speak his mind, 2. we were not willing to bring in the English custom of ministers performing the solemnity of marriage, which sermons at such times might induce, but if any minister were present, and would bestow a word of exhortation &c. it was permitted."

I have thus gleaned from Winthrop, all the facts which his valuable journal contains, relating in any manner to the military difficulties in this town, and to the conduct of the most prominent individuals concerned in them.

The dispassionate reader, while he will give to Winthrop all the credit to which his impartiality entitles him, cannot fail to discover some circumstances which tend to extenuate the criminality of the conduct of a large and respectable portion of the inhabitants of this town. The convictions which the deputy governor entertained, of the disorderly and seditious course of Mr. Hobart and his friends, were deep and strong; and in some instances his conduct indicated any thing but a charitable spirit towards those whose principal errour (if any) consisted in their attachment to more liberal views of government, than those generally entertained at that time.

Winthrop acknowledges, that " the great questions that troubled the country, were about the authority of the magistrates and the liberty of the people." "Two of the magistrates and many of the deputies" esteemed for piety, prudence and justice, " were of opinion that the magistrates exercised too much power, and that the people's liberty was thereby in danger," and the tendency of their principles and conduct was, (in the opinion of the deputy governour,) to have brought the commonwealth " to a mere democracy."

Thus we learn that one of the military company here, professed " he would die at the sword's point, if he might not have the choice of his own officers." Some of the principles and privileges for which our fathers contended, were undoubtedly too liberal and republican for the spirit of the age in which they lived. They were, perhaps, injudicious and indiscreet in their endeavours to promote their views ; and probably in some instances might not have expressed that respect for the constituted authorities, to which their character entitled them. The most superficial reader, however, may discover in the conduct of the deputy governour something of the spirit of bigotry which was, unfortunately, too often allowed to affect the judgments of the wisest and best of men at that time, and which operated very much to the injury of those who entertained more liberal opinions in politics and religion. The deputies, although conscious of the disorder which the prevalence of such principles might cause in the community, did not feel so strong a disregard of the motives of the people of Hingham, which impelled them to the course which they pursued, as to induce them to consent to impose on them heavy fines, without great reluctance.

The deputy governour appears to have been very sensitive on the subject of innovations upon the authority of government, and strongly bent, not only upon punishing, but desirous of publicly disgracing the "profane" people of Hingham. He seems to have "engulphed Bible, Testament and all, into the common law," as authority for the severe measures which were taken to mortify their feelings and to check the spread of principles so democratic in their tendency, and so dangerous to the interests of the commonwealth. Accordingly, we find that the magistrates sent to Mr. Hobart to forbear delivering a discourse on the occasion of the marriage of one of his church, at Boston, among other reasons, "because he was a bold man, and would speak his mind."

The effect of this controversy does not appear to have been ultimately injurious to the most conspicuous individuals engaged in it. Mr. Hobart, the pastor of Hingham, enjoyed the esteem of his people, and as has been before remarked, was relieved from the severe penalties which he incurred, by the liberality of the people of the town. His brother Joshua was afterwards frequently a deputy, and in 1674, he was honoured by an election to the office of Speaker to the House of Deputies.

It is to be admitted that the excitement necessarily caused by the agitation of this business, served to retard the growth and prosperity of the town; and while the effects of the displeasure of the government were operating to its injury, many of the inhabitants removed to other places.

In 1645, the relative wealth of several towns may be

learned from the apportionment of the public rate for that year.*

This town does not appear to have suffered much from the Indians. We find, however, that precautions were taken against their incursions, and that in 1645, June 29, a vote was taken "to erect a palisadoe around the meeting house," to prevent an assault from them. Considerable attention was paid to the maintenance of a military force ; and, among others, there are the following votes respecting the troops :

"January 1st, 1653. It is ordered and agreed upon by a joint consent of the town, that upon all general trainings either at *Boston,* or if the company meet with any other town to exercise, that then, every musketeer shall have one pound of powder allowed him by the town to shoot."

"1655, March 20. By a joint consent and general vote of the town, Capt. Joshua Hubbard is freed from paying any rates for the public charge of the town during the time that he is chief officer of the town for the exercise of the military company ;"† and in 1659 it was "ordered and agreed upon by the town that Stephen Lincoln should have twenty shillings the year to maintain his drum."

* It was as follows, viz.: Boston, £100 ; Ipswich, £61 10 ; Charlestown, £55 ; Salem, £45 ; Cambridge, £45 ; Dorchester, £43 17 6 ; Watertown, £41 05 ; Roxbury, £37 10 ; Lynn, £25 ; Newbury, £23 ; Dedham, £20 ; Concord, £15 ; Rowley, £15 ; Hingham, £15 ; Sudbury, £11 05 ; Weymouth, £10 10 ; Braintree, £10 10 ; Salisbury, £10 ; Hampton, £10 ; Medford, £7 ; Woburn, £7 ; Gloucester, £4 17 6 ; Wenham, £3 10,—*Winthrop*, *vol.* 2, *p.* 246.

† January 1, 1660. Those whose names are hereafter mentioned do dissent from having Capt. Hubbard freed from paying his rates to the public charge of the town for the maintenance of the ministry. Nathaniel Baker, John Otis, Michael Peirce, John Jacob, William Sprague, John Tucker, sen. John Tucker, jr. William Johns : Thomas Leavitt, Onesiphorus Marsh, Joseph Jones, Henry Chamberlin, William Hersey.—*Town Records.*

In 1662 I find the following order adopted by the selectmen.* "No Indian shall set up a wigwam, either upon property of the town's common, or dwell in one already set up, from midsummer, next, until the last day of September, following, upon penalty of twenty shillings for every such offence, and if any Englishman shall give leave and permit any such wigwam to be built upon his land, he shall be liable unto the same forfeiture, and any man in the town, aggrieved, is hereby empowered to prosecute this order, and to have consideration allowed him by the selectmen."

In 1665 the inhabitants thought it expedient to procure a deed of the township from the Indians, of which a copy may be found in the appendix.

In 1666, September 10, instructions were given to the deputies of the town in the general court.† They certainly indicate that a spirit of loyalty was prevalent among the inhabitants. They were as follows :

"By   of the signification of his majesty's pleasure lately sent over to the council, we perceive how evilly represented by (to) his majesty the late proceedings of this colony with those Honourable Commissioners sent hither have been ; and that his majesty apprehends by such proceedings that those that govern this Colony doe upon the matter believe, that his majesty hath no jurisdiction over us, yea also, of serving his majesty's command, sertayne persons upon their allegiance, to appear in England, and two or three other persons to be sent, by the council, to attend his majesty, to the end his majesty in person, may heare and finally determine all matters.

---

* The selectmen were Joshua Hobart, John Thaxter, John Jacob, Thomas Lincoln, husbandman, Josiah Hobart.
† The delegates were Joshua Hobart and John Thaxter.

"Now whereas a general court is summoned upon this signification of his majesty by order of the deputy governor, as appeares by warrant signed by his secretary : We the inhabitants of Hingham judge it meet to order and instruct you our deputies, being the present representatives in the general court, to act for us, and on our behalf, amply and fully, according to his majesty's signification ; and not seemingly under any couller or pretence whatsoever, to doe or act any thing agaynst the command of his majesty and sovereigne, soe that it may appeare unto all persons, that we are not such as disowne his majesty's jurisdiction over us, but accordingly to our duty we truly acknowledge ourselves his majesty's loyal subjects and liege people.

MATTHEW HAWKE, *Town Clerk*,
*in the name and behalf of the
freemen of Hingham.*

In 1669, Nathaniel Beal was chosen by the selectmen "to keep an ordinary and to sell *sack* and *strong water* in the town of Hingham, by retail.*

In 1670, the town voted to make three divisions of the undivided common land at Conohasset, among the proprietors. The first and second divisions were made by drawing for lots, December 6th, 1670, and the third was completed March 10, 1670–1.† About the time of these

* Twenty years previous to this date—in 1649, Daniel Cushing was chosen by the town to keep an ordinary and to sell *wine* and *beer.*

† The following list of surnames of the proprietors of these lots, contains some not before mentioned. They were Joy, Andrews, Ripley, Marsh, Nichols, Thaxter, Hobart, Lane, Canterbury, (or Cantleberry) Lincoln, Sprague, Johnson, Fearing, Cushing, Burton, Chubbuck, Beal, Langlee, Mackfarlin, Jones, Bates, Peck, Prince, Baker, James, Barnes, Pitts, Leavitt, Lazell, Wilder, Chamberlin, Hewit, Pearse, Church, Stowell, Ward, Gibbs, Woodcock, Gill,

divisions, it is supposed that a few families settled within the limits of Conohasset.*

There is nothing in our records, worthy of particular notice in this department of our history, until the year 1675 when Philip, of Pokanoket, commenced the war which desolated New England. In that year, it appears that " souldiers were impressed into the country service," and disbursements were made by the selectmen, to defray their expenses. The town suffered in some degree from the incursions of the Indians.

Thus we find in Hobart's Diary that on the 19th of April, 1676, " John Jacob† (was) slain by the Indians near his father's house," and the next day, " Joseph Joanes's‡ and Anthony Sprague's houses burnt, also,

Burr, Hawke, Jacob, Tucker, Farrow, Loring, Stodder, Hughs, Huit, Whiton, Tower, Mansfield, Smith, Bacon's heirs, Dunbar, and Otis.

* Mr. Flint's Discourses.

† John Jacob went out with his musket to shoot the deer that trespassed upon a field of wheat, near the place where the meeting house at Glad Tidings Plain is now situated. The Indians, who had secreted themselves in that neighborhood the night previous, discovered and shot Jacob, near the field of wheat. He was found dead, and his musket was battered to pieces. This traditionary account, has been related to me by Mr. Joseph Wilder, now living. Another traditionary account states, that Jacob was a famous hunter, and made a declaration that he never would be taken alive by the Indians, and that when found, his friends were rejoiced that he was not taken alive, as well as that he was not carried into captivity, to be put to death by Indian tortures ; and that the rock where he was found, was, in allusion to this event, called Glad Tidings Rock," the same from which the name "Glad Tidings Plain," originated. Mr. Wilder, whose narration is clear, and I am inclined to think the most correct, states that he was not found at the rock, now called " Glad Tidings Rock," but that this name originated from the fact, that a woman who had strayed away from home and was supposed to be lost, was first discovered from this rock. The correctness of this tradition is scarcely questionable.

‡ The houses of Joseph Joanes and Anthony Sprague were situated at the place called " Over the River," that of the latter, near where Mr. Gilbert now lives.

Israel Hobart's, Nathaniel Chubbuck's, James Whiton's houses burnt down by the Indians."

In consequence of apprehensions of the depredations of Indians, the following order was adopted by the selectmen in 1676. "The selectmen of Hingham, taking into consideration the great danger we are in, and damage might ensue on us, by the Indians being our open enemies, and also complaint made to us on that account, do therefore order and agree that no person or persons in this town shall take in any Indian or Indians into the said town, or entertain or keep any Indian or Indians, in the said town or in their service or houses, without order from authority, under the penalty of twenty shillings for every such offence," &c.*

Garrison houses were established for the security of the inhabitants, but I am unable to ascertain their number and situation. There were, also, in the town three forts, but the date of their erection cannot be ascertained. One of them was situated on the hill, which at that time commanded the harbour, the same of which the mounds are still visible in the Burying Yard ;† another at the place called Fort Hill, and another "on the Plain about a mile from the Harbour." There is frequent mention of disbursements for the soldiers, in the selectmen's book of records, about this time.

It is proper in this place, to give some account of the proceedings of the town relating to the erection of a new meeting house. The first meeting house was situated, as

* Similar orders were adopted at subsequent periods.
† I am informed by Samuel Norton, Esq. that there is a tradition that "this fort was built from the fear of invasion by sea, by the Dutch, &c." This statement was made to him by Dr. Gay, the third minister of the town.

has been stated, near the spot on which the post office now stands, opposite the Academy.

By the increase of the population it became necessary to build a house of worship of larger dimensions, and accordingly we find that on the 19th of January, 1679–80, the inhabitants of the town " agreed to build a new meeting house with all convenient speed," and Capt. Joshua Hobart, Capt. John Jacob, and Ensign John Thaxter were chosen a committee to view the meeting houses of other towns, for the purposes of forming an opinion of the dimensions of a building necessary to accommodate the inhabitants, to ascertain the probable expense, and to report at the next town meeting, to be held in May following.

On the 3d of May, 1680, the selectmen were directed to " carry on the business to effect, about building a new meeting house ;" and at the same meeting it was voted " to have the new meeting house set up, in the place where the old one doth now stand."*

This vote was not carried into effect ; but the house was eventually erected (not without opposition,) on the

---

* Those who voted in favour of erecting the new meeting house on the place where the old one stood, were the following, viz. : Capt. Joshua Hobart, John Beal, sen. Dea. John Leavitt, Andrew Lane, Thomas Gill, sen. John Beal, Edward Wilder, Doctor Cutler, Ens. John Thaxter, Thomas Lincoln, husbandman, Nathaniel Beal, sen. Edmund Pitts, Joshua Lincoln, Thomas Marsh, Francis James, Stephen Lincoln, Moses Collier, John Prince, John Langlee, Joshua Beal, Thomas Lincoln, carpenter, Caleb Beal, James Hersey, Thomas Andrews, Joseph Joy, William Hersey, Matthias Briggs, John Chubbuck, Josiah Lane, Robert Waterman, Matthew Whiton, Serg. Daniel Lincoln, Samuel Stowell—33. Those who voted in the negative on this question were the following, viz. : Daniel Cushing, sen. Nathaniel Baker, Joseph Jacob, Humphrey Johnson, Capt. John Jacob, Serg. Matthew Cushing, Simon Burr, sen. James Whiton, Ibrook Tower, Lt. John Smith, Jeremiah Beal, sen.—11.

hill where it now stands. Mr. Flint, in his century sermons, speaks of the "violent contest in regard to the placing of a meeting house, in which the interference of the *general court* was required."*

On the 11th of August 1680, the dimensions of the house were fixed by a vote of the town as follows,—length fifty five feet, breadth forty five feet, and the height of the posts "twenty or one and twenty feet;" with galleries on one side and at both ends. In 1681, May 2, the town approved of what the selectmen had done in relation to the building of the new meeting house, and the place where it was to be set.†

May 24, 1681, the town voted to set the meeting house on the most convenient place, on the land of Capt. Joshua Hobart. In this situation it now stands. The house was raised on the 26th, 27th and 28th days of July, 1681, and it cost the town £430 and the old house.‡ In 1681-2, January 8, the inhabitants first met for public worship in the new house.§

* There is a tradition, and I confess not a very plausible one, that the site for the meeting house was fixed on the Lower Plain,—that the day was appointed for the raising of the frame, but that on the preceding night, it was carrried to the spot where the meeting house now stands. And it has been further stated, that the party on the Plain condescended that it should be placed where it now is. I can scarcely credit this tradition. There is no record of a vote fixing the site on the Plain, in the town records; besides it is scarcely to be presumed that one party would have resisted the authority of a vote of the town, if such an one had been passed; or that the other party with the advantage of such a vote, would have quietly yielded to an infraction of their rights.

† 37 persons dissented from this vote.
‡ Hobart's Diary.
§ Two additions have been made to the building, the first about the year 1730, and the second in 1755. These additions were made, however, without materially altering the external appearance and form of the house. It is yet in a good state of preservation, and its frame of oak, bears no marks of dilapidation or decay.

Although the controversy respecting the location of the meeting-house, was the cause of considerable excitement among the inhabitants ; it does not appear to have continued for any great length of time. It was nearly forty years from this period, when the east precinct was established ; and from this fact, we infer that the excitement happily subsided, or measures would have been taken at a much earlier date, to have erected another house of worship.

In 1682, at a meeting of the military company for the nomination of officers to be presented to the General Court for approbation, James Hawke received a majority of the votes given for an Ensign ; but it appears from the following copy of a remonstrance against his appointment to the office, that there was some irregularity in the proceedings of the company, which required the interposition of the General Court.

The petition is as follows :

" *To the honoured General Court sitting in Boston the* 11 : *of October* 1682.

" We whose names are hereunto subscribed, doe hereby acquaint your honours that in our Town, there lately passed a vote amongst our foote company of souldjers, for nomination of military officers to present to this honoured Court ; Lieutenant John Smith was nominated for Captain, Ensign Jeremiah Beale for Lieutenant ; and for Ensign, Sergant Thomas Andrewes had forty seven votes and James Hawk had fifty five, the yonger sort of persons were for James Hawk, the said James Hawk is a yong man and never was in any office, but a private souldjer. Sergant Thomas Andrewes is a good souldjer and we doubt not but is well known to many of the members of this Honoured Court, and we humbly desire if your honours please he might be allowed of; our reasons for our request are, first, otherwise we shall not have any Commission officer but will be remote from the center of the Town, and another reason is, we plainly perceive and undoubtedly know, that there will be much discontent amongst the souldjers if James Hawk be allowed of, we are yours to serve and shall always pray for your Honours' happiness as in duty we are bound.

"We whose names are hereunder written were not at the abovesaid nomination, nor had any notice of it but desire Sergant Thomas Andrewes may be allowed of for Ensign if your Honours please."

Signed by Enoch Hobart and twenty-three others.*

At the October Court, 1682, the following order was passed, viz :

"In answer to the petition of several inhabitants of Hingham, the Court, taking notice of the irregular and illegal proceedings of the military foot company of the said town, as to the election of their commission officers, do declare their dissatisfaction therewith, and do expect the acknowledgement of their error and offence therein, for the present do direct and order the commission officers of said company to manage the affairs thereof to all intents till this Court take further order."

At the special court, in February and March after, Lieutenant John Smith was appointed Captain, Jeremiah

---

* The other signatures were, Benjamin Garnet, John Lane, Paul Gilford, John Record, Ebenezer Plumb, John Low, Matthew Whyton, John Bull, Josiah Lowring, Simon Gross, John Beale, senior, Thomas Hobart, Edmond Pitts, William Hersey, senior, Caleb Beale, Joshua Lincoln, Jacob Beale, Steven Lincoln, John Beale, junior, John Fering, Joseph Bate, Samuel Bate, Thomas Gill.

[The orthography of Daniel Cushing is preserved in the petition and signatures.]

Beal, Lieutenant, and Thomas Lincoln, Ensign, of the foot company in Hingham. As an individual was appointed who was the candidate of neither party, I conclude that there was a compromise of the difficulty ; and as our records contain nothing more relating to the matter, it is presumed that this appointment ended the dispute.

In 1690, Hingham furnished a portion of her citizens to join the expedition to Canada, under the command of Sir William Phips. " Captain Thomas Andrews and soldiers went on board ship to go to Canada," on the 6th of August of that year. The fleet sailed for Quebec on the 9th of August.* Capt. Andrews, and most of the soldiers belonging to this town, died in the expedition.† ‡

In 1702, Hingham was divided into two foot companies.§

I have examined a list of the rateable estate in this town, in 1749, made by Benjamin Lincoln, Abel Cushing, Samuel Cushing, Ebenezer Beal and John Thaxter, As-

*Cushing's MSS.

† " Capt. Thomas Andrews, John Chubbuck, Jonathan Burr, Jonathan May, Daniel Tower, —— Judkins, Samuel Gilford and two more, died of the Small Pox in the Canada expedition, and one slain."—*Hobart's Diary.*

‡ In 1690 by the selectmen's book of records, it appears, that on the 25th of December of that year, a rate was made by the selectmen, amounting to £57,7,8. And among the disbursements are the following items, viz. :

" To Enoch Whiting, for killing two wolves, £1,00,0
To John Lincoln, for drumming, 2,10,0."

In 1691-2, the rate was £64,9,4. In the disbursements, there are several items for drumming and for killing wolves, and some for money paid to soldiers. The minister's salary was not paid out of these rates. It was eighty five pounds. In 1698, the rate made for the maintenance of the ministry, school, poor, &c. was £130, and the price of grain was fixed as follows ; Indian corn, 3s. per bushel ; barley, 3s. ; rye, 3s. 6d., and oats 1s. 6d.

§ Hobart's Diary.

sessors, from which it appears, that there were in this town at that time, seven grist, fulling, and saw mills, *two chaises and three chairs*, six hundred and sixty three acres of tillage land, one hundred and fifty one acres of orchard, two thousand and forty three acres of mowing land, two hundred and forty tons of vessels engaged in foreign trade, one hundred and seven tons of open vessels, and one hundred and sixteen tons of decked vessels.

During fifty years, subsequent to 1700, the town records contain nothing worthy of particular notice, excepting what has already been mentioned. The affairs of the town, during that period, appear to have been conducted with order and discretion. In the wars between the English and the French and Indians, many of the citizens of Hingham enlisted. In 1757, at the capitulation of Fort William Henry, there were present from this town, Major Samuel Thaxter, Thomas Gill, Thomas Burr, Elijah Lewis, Knight Sprague, and Seth Stowers. All of them fortunately escaped the barbarous massacre which ensued. Major Thaxter was then an officer, (I think a Captain,) and with the others, was stripped of his clothing and very narrowly escaped with life. Jeremiah Lincoln and a person by the name of Lathrop, from this town, were out in the same expedition, and were taken prisoners in a scouting party previously to the capitulation. Lathrop was killed, and Jeremiah Lincoln* was carried into captivity to Canada, where he remained for a considerable time, and afterwards made his escape, and returned in safety to his native town.

* Jeremiah Lincoln was an Iron Smith. He died in Lunenburg, Massachusetts. Two of his apprentices were the late Lt. Gov. Lincoln, of Worcester, and Dr. Peter Hobart, of Hanover, both of whom left his service, for the purpose of obtaining an education at Harvard University.

Knight Sprague* was, in 1826, the only survivor of those who engaged in this expedition from Hingham.

Capt. Joshua Barker, of this town, served as a Lieutenant under Capt. Winslow, in the expedition to the West Indies in 1740, and in the different wars of the country from 1742 to 1758.†

I come now to an interesting period in the history of this town; a period upon which our venerable fathers who participated in the toils, sufferings and dangers of the AMERICAN REVOLUTION, can look back with plea-

---

* Knight Sprague is mentioned in the history of Leicester, written by Emory Washburn, Esq. and published in June, 1826. The following extract is from that history:

"One man yet survives, at the advanced age of 86 who was a soldier from 1756 to 1761, and was in the memorable affair of Fort William Henry, in 1757, when so many English and Americans were massacred by the savages of Montcalm's army. His name is Knight Sprague, a native of Hingham, from which place he marched, in 1756. The next year, he was with Col. Bradstreet at the taking of Fort Frontinac, on Lake Ontario. His memory is yet accurate and tenacious. Fort William Henry was surrendered, according to his account, about 10 o'clock on Wednesday morning, and the English were detained till the next morning and guarded by the French. As soon however as the army had left the fort, to take up their march, according to the terms of capitulation, the Indians rushed upon them, and began to strip and kill the prisoners. Sprague escaped, after being partially stripped. His captain was stripped naked, as were many women he passed, in his flight towards Fort Edward. Of the half company to which he belonged, fifteen out of the fifty, were killed, that day. Munro, the British commander, as represented by Sprague, was a dignified man of about fifty years of age. Montcalm was a fine looking man, extremely well formed, and very active and graceful, but small in stature."

† N. H. Historical Collections, vol. ii, p. 221, where the name is erroneously printed *Warner*.

Capt. Barker died January 1, 1785, in the 74th year of his age. In an obituary notice of him, he is described as an excellent and brave officer, and a man of real worth, "respectful to his superiors, easy and familiar to his inferiors, and good to all; in his address courteous and graceful, in his temper calm and serene," beloved in life and lamented in death.

sure and pride ; and in which those acts of patriotism and daring and successful achievement were performed, which entitle them to the gratitude and veneration of all posterity. A distinguished orator has said, that " Any one who has had occasion to be acquainted with the records of the New England towns, knows well how to estimate those merits and those sufferings. Nobler records of patriotism exist no where. No where can there be found higher proofs of a spirit that was ready to hazard all, to pledge all, to sacrifice all, in the cause of the country. The voice of Otis and of Adams in Faneuil Hall, found its full and true echo in the little councils of the interior towns ; and if, within the Continental Congress, patriotism shone more conspicuously, it did not there exist more truly, nor burn more fervently ; it did not render the day more anxious or the night more sleepless ; it sent up no more ardent prayer to God for succour ; and it put forth, in no greater degree, the fulness of its effort, and the energy of its whole soul and spirit, in the common cause, than it did in the small assemblies of the towns."

The remarks are as just as they are elegant ; and without claiming for the citizens of this town any more merit for their zeal in promoting the great cause of their country, when contending for "liberty and the pursuit of happiness," than others are entitled to, their records certainly indicate that no where did patriotism put forth in "a greater degree, the fulness of its efforts and the energy of its whole soul and spirit."

In the events which preceded the American Revolution, the inhabitants felt and expressed a deep interest. I shall certainly be excused for presenting copious extracts from the Town Records, that a correct opinion may be formed of the motives which actuated the conduct of our fathers.

and of the bold and determined spirit which dictated their patriotic resolutions. And this I do, as the best method of exhibiting the character of those individuals who gave a tone to public sentiment ; and whose merits for their devotion to the cause of their country, cannot be too conspicuously displayed.

At the annual March meeting in 1768, the town chose a committee to devise measures for the encouragement of industry and economy, and to report at the next May meeting. The committee was composed of the following gentlemen, viz : Hon. Benjamin Lincoln,* John Thaxter, Esq. Capt. Theophilus Cushing, Dea. Joshua Hersey, Dr. Ezekiel Hersey, Caleb Bates, Capt. Daniel Lincoln, Capt. Joseph Thaxter, Lazarus Beal, and Dea. Isaac Lincoln.

The committee reported in May as follows :

" The committee appointed by the town of Hingham, at their meeting in March last, to take under consideration the encouraging and promoting economy and industry in the said town, report the following Resolves. First, that we will by all ways and means in our power encourage and promote the practice of virtue, and suppressing of vice and immorality, the latter of which seem daily increasing among us, and the decay of the former much to be lamented. (*This part of the first paragraph being read, the question was put whether it be accepted ; passed in the affirmative.*) And for promoting the one and discourag-

---

* Hon. Benjamin Lincoln, the father of Gen. Benjamin Lincoln, of the army of the revolution. " He was a member of his Majesty's Council from the year 1753 to 1770, when he resigned his seat at the board. In various offices of public trust, as well as in those of private life, he served his generation with uncommon diligence and exemplary fidelity. He died March 1, 1771, in the 72d year of his age."—*Fleets' Boston Evening Post.*

ing the other, we apprehend the lessening the number of licensed houses, would greatly contribute to the purpose and that not more than three retailers in the North Parish, two in the East and one in the South, would be as many as would be consistent with the interests of the community. (*This remaining part of the first paragraph being read, the question was put whether it be accepted ; passed in the negative.*) Secondly, we resolve for the future, to improve our lands more generally for raising of flax, and increasing our stocks of sheep, which materials properly improved among ourselves may prevent the necessity of using so great a quantity of imported commodities and increasing our own manufactures, and thereby the poorer sort more profitably employed, the medium likewise, in a great measure preserved and increased, for the want of which the industrious are at this time under great disadvantages. (*This second resolve being read, the question was put whether the same be accepted ; passed in the affirmative.*)"

The adoption of the above resolutions was in accordance with the spirit of others approved and adopted at Boston, and in other places.

The following is a copy of the proceedings of the town on the 21st of September, 1768, on the reception of a circular from the inhabitants of Boston :

"At the said meeting the town chose Dea. Joshua Hearsey a committee, to join the committees from the several towns within the province, to assemble at Boston on the 22d day of September, current, then and there to consult such measures as shall be necessary for the preservation of good order and regularity in the province at this critical conjuncture of affairs, and voted the following instructions to him, viz. :

"As you are chosen and appointed by the town of Hingham, to join with committees from the several towns within this Province, desired to meet at Boston on the 22d day of September, current, then and there to consult such measures as shall be necessary for the preservation of good order and regularity in the Province, at this critical conjuncture of affairs. We advise and direct you that you use your endeavors to preserve peace and good order, in the Province and loyalty to the king ; that you take every legal and constitutional method for the preservation of our rights and liberties, and for having redressed those grievances, we so generally complain of and so sensibly feel ; that all possible care be taken that the troops, (that) should arrive, have provision made for them, so that they be not billeted in private families and at so convenient a distance as not to interrupt the people ; that you encourage the inhabitants to keep up military duty whereby they may be in a capacity to defend themselves against foreign enemies ; and in case you are exposed to any charges in prosecuting any of the foregoing preparations, we will repay it, and as these instructions are for your private use, improve them for that purpose and for no other whatever.

"The foregoing instructions were drawn up by Dr. Ezekiel Hearsey, Benjamin Lincoln, jr. and Capt. Daniel Lincoln."

The committees from the several towns met agreeably to appointment on the 22d of September. Sixty six towns, besides districts, were represented, by upwards of seventy gentlemen. The number afterwards increased to above one hundred, from ninety eight towns and districts. Their debates and proceedings were open. The convention continued their session every day till the 29th, (although admonished by Gov. Bernard to break up and separate themselves,) and during that time they adopted a letter to be transmitted to the agent of the province at London, and published a " result of their conference and consultation," in which they declared their allegiance to the king, their abhorrence of riots, and their determination to yield all assistance to the civil magistrates towards suppressing them, and also declared their rights by charter and by nature and their humble dependance on their gracious sovereign, that their wrongs would be speedily redressed."*

In 1770, March 19, the inhabitants of Hingham passed resolutions relating to the non-consumption of imported goods, and to the Boston massacre. These resolutions do not appear in the town records, but are contained in the following letter from Gen. Lincoln to the committee of merchants in Boston.

To the Gentlemen the Committee of Merchants in Boston.

HINGHAM, MARCH 24th, 1770.

"GENTLEMEN—At the annual meeting of the town of Hingham, on the 19th day of March, A. D. 1770 : Upon a motion being made and seconded (though omitted in the warrant) the inhabitants taking into consideration the distressed circumstances of the people in this and the neighbouring Provinces, occasioned by the late parliamentary acts for raising a revenue in North America, the manner of collecting the same, and the measures gone into to enforce obedience to them, and judging that every society and every individual person are loudly called to exert the utmost of their abillity in a constitutional way to procure a redress of those grievances, and to secure the privileges

* Snow's History of Boston.

by charter conveyed to them, and that freedom which they have a right to as men and English subjects, came to the following votes :

"Voted, That we highly approve of the patriotic resolutions of the merchants of this Province not to import goods from Great Britain till the repeal of the aforesaid acts, and viewing it as having a tendency to retrieve us from those burthens so much complained of, and so sensibly felt by us; we will do all in our power, in a legal way, to support them in carrying into execution so worthy an undertaking.

"Voted, That those few who have imported goods contrary to general agreement and counteracted the prudent and laudable efforts of the merchants and traders aforesaid, have thereby forfeited the confidence of their brethren; and therefore, we declare that we will not directly or indirectly have any commerce or dealings with them.

"Voted, That we will discourage the use of foreign superfluities among us and encourage our own manufactures.

"Voted, That we heartily sympathize with our brethren of the town of Boston, in the late unhappy destruction of so many of their inhabitants, and we rejoice with them that there yet remains the free exercise of the civil authority.

"Voted, That the town clerk be ordered to transmit a copy hereof to the Committee of Merchants in Boston.

"I cheerfully comply with the above order and herewith send you a copy of the Votes.

"I am, gentlemen, with great esteem, your most obedient and most humble servant.

BENJAMIN LINCOLN, Jun'r."

The frequency of town meetings, at this period, and the inconvenience to which the inhabitants of Conohasset were subject in transacting their civil concerns in Hingham induced them to apply to the goverment, for an act of incorporation as a town. The petition was granted and the east or second precinct was incorporated a town, April 26, 1770, by the name of Cohasset.*

The views and feelings of the inhabitants of this town, respecting the subjects of controversy between this and the mother country, may be learned from the following instructions given to their representative to the General Court:

" The committee chosen to draft some instructions proper to be given our representative reported as followeth; We the subscribers being appointed by the inhabitants of the town of Hingham, at a legal meeting on the 11th inst. and to draft some instructions proper to be given our representative under the present alarming situation of affairs in this government, beg leave to report as followeth, viz: *To John Thaxter, Esq.*

" Whereas your constituents are feelingly sensible of a number of infringements on their rights and privileges until lately unheard of, the whole of which we pretend not to enumerate to you as from your knowledge of our present state, they must bear strongly on your own mind; but would notwithstanding mention the following: First, the act of Parliament passed in the last session thereof, entitled an act for the better preserving his Majesty's dock-yards, magazines, ships, ammunition and stores, we look upon to be one of the greatest grievances, that persons accused of capital offences should be carried 3000 miles distant from the place where the crime was com-

* Flint's Century Discourses.

mitted, to be tried, the inconvenience and injustice of which so fully appear that there needs no animadversion. Second, The act of Parliament obliging all ships or vessels from Portugal to this province, to enter their fruit in some port of Great Britain, by which great expense must arise, and the fruit often much damaged, by which means the trade is burthened, clogged and discouraged,—we on the whole instruct you, that you use your utmost endeavours, by dispassionate remonstrance, and humble petition in a legislative way, to the Parliament of Great Britain, to have these and all grievances, we now labour under, redressed, and those we fear from circumstances are taking place.

"And we instruct you, that you use your best endeavours, that a salary be granted by this province to the Judges of the Superior Court, as shall be adequate to their important office ; and that you endeavour that a harmony may subsist on a proper foundation between the several branches of the legislative body of this province, which cement is essentially necessary to the interest and happiness thereof.

     Bela Lincoln,
     Benjamin Lincoln,
     Joseph Thaxter, } Committee.
     Jacob Cushing,
     Joshua Hearsey,
Hingham, January 13, 1773."

1774, January 31. The town appointed a committee to take into consideration a letter and papers sent from the Boston Committee of Correspondence to this town. The committee was composed of the following gentlemen: Benjamin Lincoln, Esq. Joseph Andrews, Dea. Joshua Hersey, Dea. Theophilus Cushing, Caleb Bates, James Fearing, Jacob Cushing, Esq. Thomas Loring, and Hezekiah Cushing. They presented a report at the annual town meeting in March following, from which the nature of the subjects submitted to their consideration, fully appears. It was as follows :

"When we call to mind a late Act of the British Parliament, expressly declaring that the King, Lords and Commons, in Parliament assembled, have ever had, and of right ought to have, full power and authority to make laws and statutes of sufficient force and validity to bind the colonies and people of America, subject to the Crown of Great Britain, in all cases whatever, and in consequence thereof an Act of Parliament made for the express purpose of raising a revenue in America, for defraying the charge of the administration of justice &c. in the colonies ; and when also we consider that the more effectually to carry into execution the same Act, the councils of the nation, in a late session of the British Parliament, have empowered the East India Company to export their teas to America, free of all duties in England, but still liable to a duty on its being landed in the colonies ; and comparing those Acts and others similar to them, with several clauses in the charter granted to this province by their late Majesties, King William and Queen Mary, of blessed memory, in which it is among other things ordained and established that all and every of the subjects of us, our heirs and successors, which shall go to inhabit in our said province and territory, and every of their children which shall happen to be born there, or on the seas going thither or returning from thence, shall have and enjoy all the liberties and immunities of free and natural subjects, within any of the dominions of us, our heirs and successors, to all intents, constructions and purposes whatever, as if they and every of them were born within this our realm of England, and whereas it is by the said royal charter especially ordained, that the great and general court or assembly, therein constituted, shall have full power and authority to impose and levy proportionate and reasonable assessments and taxes upon the estates and persons of all and every of the proprietors and inhabitants of the said province and territory for the service of the King, in the necessary defence and support of his government of the province, and the protection and preservation of his subjects therein; the design and tendency of which appear in too conspicuous a light to need any comment, and are too alarming to admit of silence, as silence may be construed into acquiescence. We therefore resolve,

"First, That the disposal of their property is the inherent right of freemen; that there is no property in that which another can of right take from us without our consent; that the claim of Parliament to tax America, is, in other words, a claim of right to lay contributions on us at pleasure.

"Secondly, That the duty imposed by Parliment upon tea landed in America, is a tax on the Americans or levying contributions on them without their consent.

"Thirdly, That the express purpose for which the tax is levied on the Americans, viz.: for the support of government and administration of justice, and the defence of his majesty's dominions in America, has a direct tendency to render assemblies useless, and to introduce arbitrary government and slavery.

"Fourthly, That a virtuous and steady opposition to the ministerial plan of governing America, is necessary to preserve even a shadow of liberty; and is a duty which every freeman in America, owes to his country, to himself and to his posterity.

"Fifthly, That the resolution lately come into by the East India Company, to send out their teas to America subject to the payment of duties on its being landed here, is an open attempt to enforce the ministerial plan, and a violent attack on the liberties of America.

"Sixthly, That it is the duty of every American to oppose this attempt.

"Seventhly, That it affords the greatest satisfaction to the inhabitants of this town, to find that his majesty's subjects in the American colonies, and of this Province in particular, are so thoroughly awakened to a sense of their danger, arising from encroachments made on their constitutional rights and liberties, and that so firm a union is established among them; and that they will ever be ready to join their fellow subjects in all laudable measures for the redress of the many grievances we labour under.

"After the said report having been several times read, upon a motion made, the question was put, whether the same be accepted and be recorded in the town's book of records and a copy thereof sent by the town clerk, to the Committee of Correspondence of the town of Boston; and it passed in the affirmative."

In 1774, August 17, the town adopted the following agreement* as reported by a committee, but stayed all farther proceedings until the report of the Continental Congress:

"We the subscribers taking into our serious consideration the present distressed state of America, and in particular of this devoted Province, occasioned by several

* This agreement or covenant was reported by a committee consisting of the following gentlemen, viz.: Dea. Joshua Hersey, Col. Benjamin Lincoln, Dea. Theophilus Cushing, Dea. Benjamin Cushing, Mr. Samuel Norton, Mr. Joseph Andrews, Mr. Israel Beal, Jacob Cushing, Esq. Mr. Enoch Lincoln, Mr. Heman Lincoln, Mr. Thomas Loring, Capt. —— Jones, Mr. James Fearing, Mr. Jabez Wilder, jr., Mr. Hezekiah Cushing.

late unconstitutional acts of the British Parliament for taxing Americans without their consent—blocking up the port of Boston—vacating our charter, that solemn compact between the king and the people, respecting certain laws of this Province, heretofore enacted by our general court and confirmed by his majesty and his predecessors. We feel ourselves bound as we regard our inestimable constitution, and the duty we owe to succeeding generations, to exert ourselves in this peaceably way, to recover our lost and preserve our remaining privileges, yet not without grief for the distresses that may hereby be brought upon our brethren in Great Britain, we solemnly covenant and engage to and with each other, viz. :

"1st. That we will not import, purchase, or consume, nor suffer any person or persons to, by, for or under us to import, purchase, or consume in any manner whatever, any goods, wares or merchandize which shall arrive in America, from Great Britain, from and after the first day of October, one thousand seven hundred and seventy four, until our charter and constitutional rights shall be restored ; or until it shall be determined by the major part of our brethren in this and the neighbouring colonies, that a non importation, or a non consumption agreement will not effect the desired end ; or until it shall be apparent that a non importation, or non consumption agreement will not be entered into by this and the neighbouring colonies, except drugs and medicines, and such articles, and such only, as will be absolutely necessary in carrying on our own manufactures.

"2dly. That in order to prevent, as far as in us lies, any inconveniences that may arise from the disuse of foreign commodities ; we agree that we will take the most prudent care for the raising and preserving sheep, flax, &c. for the manufacturing all such woollen and linen cloths as shall be most useful and necessary ; and that we will give all possible support and encouragement to the manufactures of America in general."

1774, September 21. (Col.) Benjamin Lincoln was chosen to attend a Provincial Congress at Concord. In October, 1774, the town "recommended to the militia officers to assemble their men once in a week, and instruct them in the art of war, &c." In November, the collectors of taxes were directed to pay all monies collected to Henry Gardner, Esq. of Stow, appointed treasurer by the Provincial Congress.

December 26, 1774, Benjamin Lincoln was chosen to represent the town in the Provincial Congress to be held at Cambridge, in the ensuing February ; and on the same day, a committee was appointed to draft a petition to the clergymen, requesting them, if they thought it consistent with their duty, to encourage the people to comply with the *association* so called of the Continental Congress. A petition was reported by the committee and presented by another committee of nine, to Rev. Messrs. Gay and Shute. They complied with the request of the town ; each of them addressed the people, at the next town meeting, for which the town gave them a vote of thanks. In January, 1775, the town chose a committee to take into consideration the state of the militia.*

May 24, 1775, Benjamin Lincoln was chosen to represent the town in the Provincial Congress then sitting at Watertown ; and at the same meeting Benjamin Lincoln, Benjamin Cushing, and David Cushing were chosen a committee to correspond with other towns in this Province.

* Col. Lincoln, Enoch Lincoln, Jotham Loring, Samuel Norton, Jacob Leavitt, Samuel Thaxter, and Seth Stowers, composed the committee.

1775, July 10, Benjamin Lincoln was chosen to represent the town in the General Court to be held at Watertown on the 19th of that month, agreeably to a resolve of the Continental Congress. In August, Enoch Lincoln was chosen to attend the General Court then sitting.

During the year 1775, it appears by the selectmen's and town records, that money was raised and disbursements were frequently made, to improve the condition of the militia, and to provide arms and ammunition, to be used on any emergency.

1776, March 18, Theophilus Cushing, Esq. John Fearing, Thomas Loring, Israel Beal,* and Peter Hobart were chosen a Committee of Correspondence, Inspection and Safety.

On the 23d of May, Enoch Lincoln, Theophilus Cushing and John Fearing were chosen representatives to the General Court; and Benjamin Lincoln, Hezekiah Cushing, and Dea. Joshua Hersey were appointed a committee to prepare instructions for the representatives.

As the important crisis of the Declaration of Independence of the colonies approached, and with it an excitement which extended universally throughout the country; when the repeated aggressions of Great Britain upon the rights of the colonies had roused a spirit of

---

* There are few men whose characters present more to admire, than that of Mr. Israel Beal. Destitute of the advantages of an early education, he possessed a strength of mind, and a soundness of judgment which peculiarly qualified him for the important duties of a member of the committee of safety, and for other duties which he was frequently called upon to perform. Discreet, intelligent, and possessed of an unblemished character of honesty and integrity, he exercised an influence over the minds of men, to which others of greater advantages and more extensive acquirements could not attain. As a neighbour, a friend, a citizen, he was universally esteemed, and I hear no one speak of his excellent qualities of mind and heart, but with terms of the most sincere regard. He died in July, 1813.

indignation in some breasts, and created despondency and pusillanimity in others ; at a time when energy and decision were most needed, the following manly and independent instructions were given by the town to their representatives. They were drawn up by the committtee before mentioned.

To Enoch Lincoln, Theophilus Cushing, and John Fearing.

"GENTLEMEN—You are delegated to represent the Town of Hingham, in the next General Court, to be held in this colony ; and although we entertain the highest sense of your integrity, patriotism and ability, of which we have given full evidence in appointing you to this weighty trust, yet as matters of the greatest importance, relative to the freedom and happiness, not only of this, but of all the United Colonies, on which you may wish to have the advice of your constituents, will come before you for your determination—you are instructed and directed at all times to give your vote and interest in support of the present struggle with Great Britain ; we ask nothing of her but *"Peace, Liberty and Safety;"* you will never recede from that claim ; and agreeably to a resolve of the late House of Representatives, in case the honourable Continental Congress declare themselves *independent* of the Kingdom of Great Britain, *solemnly to engage in behalf of your constituents, that they will, with their* LIVES *and* FORTUNES, *support them in the measure.*

"You will also, as soon as may be, endeavour to procure a more equal representation of this colony in General Assembly ; and that it be by fewer members, than at present the several towns have a right to return ; and when this is effected you will give your vote for calling a new house.   BENJAMIN LINCOLN, *Town Clerk.*

The Committee of Correspondence, Inspection and Safety, chosen in March, 1777, were Israel Beal, Samuel

Norton, John Fearing, Peter Cushing, Thomas Loring, Peter Hobart and Theophilus Cushing.

In May, Mr. Enoch Lincoln was chosen to represent the town in the General Court. He was instructed to assist in forming a Constitution, on the condition, that it should be laid before the town " for their approbation or disapprobation, before the establishment thereof." In June following, the town reconsidered their previous vote instructing the representative, and voted, " that upon *mature deliberation,* this town direct said representative on *no terms to consent to it,* but to use his influence and oppose it heartily, if such an attempt should be made ; for we apprehend, this matter, at a suitable time will come before the people at large, to delegate a select number for that purpose, and that only ; and that he exert his influence that such body be formed as soon as may be."

The town, at this important period, was ever vigilant and watchful of its own interests and of those of the country. In June, 1777, Mr. Israel Beal, was appointed " to procure evidence against such persons as are suspected of being inimical to this and the United States of America, in this town."

In 1778, the Committee of Correspondence, &c. were Thomas Burr, Jacob Leavitt, Abel Hersey, Enoch Whiton and Peter Hobart. The representatives chosen in May, were Enoch Lincoln and Joseph Thaxter.

In June, the town voted " not to accept of the form of government proposed by the General Court, for the State of Massachusetts Bay. Fifty six votes against the proposed form of government and not one in favour of it." At the same time, instructions were given to the representative, " to use his influence that a constitution be formed, at some suitable time, *by a body chosen by the people for that purpose and that only.*"

The Committee of Correspondence, &c. in 1779, were Samuel Norton, Dr. Thomas Thaxter, Capt. Theophilus Wilder, Capt. Charles Cushing and Joseph Thaxter.

In May, Mr. Joseph Thaxter, Jr. was chosen representative to the General Court. At the same time, the views of the citizens were again expressed on the subject of a constitution. It was voted, 42 to 8, that "it is not best at this time, to have a new form of government." In July, Rev. Daniel Shute and Mr. Joseph Thaxter were chosen delegates to the convention for forming a constitution.

In 1780, the Committee of Correspondence, &c. were Israel Beal, Capt. Charles Cushing, Ebenezer Cushing, Joshua Leavitt and Isaac Wilder, Jr.

In May, a large committee was chosen "to examine the form of government proposed by the late convention," to report at the next meeting.

The committee reported as follows :

"The committee appointed to take into consideration the frame of a constitution for this state, presented to the town for their consideration and revision, by the convention appointed for preparing the same, having carefully gone through and maturely considered the said frame of a constitution, humbly offer it as our opinion ; that it is a system well calculated in general, to promote the present and future happiness of this state ; by securing to the individuals of which it is composed, safety and property ; at once guarding the rights of conscience, and making provision for the promotion of virtue and morality, each absolutely necessary to the support and good order of society ; in fine, that while it gives energy and dignity to legal authority, it equally ensures peace, liberty and safety to the subject ; yet it is an human production, and though good as a system, may possibly admit of amendment in some of its parts ; we have therefore taken the liberty to hint the following, viz. : In the article of the first section, of the 2d chapter, it is proposed that the governour be empowered, with the advice of the council, in the recess of the General Court to march or transport the inhabitants of this state, to the relief of a neighbouring state, invaded, or threatened with immediate invasion : this we owe as men, besides we are taught it by a principle of policy. It is apparent, that while time may be spent in collecting the general court, destruction may be brought upon our neighbours, and war with all its consequences come even to our own doors,—thousands of lives may be lost and millions of property expended, that by timely exertion might be saved ; add to this, the articles of confederation bind us to grant, which can only be but by vesting the governour with such power.

" In the fourth section, of the same article first, it is proposed that the time of service of the commissary general be limited to five years, except in time of war or rebellion, upon the same principle and for the same reasons that the time of service of the treasurer is limited to that time.

" Your committee recommend, that the town instruct their delegates to use their endeavours that the foregoing amendments be made ; but if that cannot be obtained, that they then accept the constitution as it now stands ; convinced of the zeal, integrity and abilities of our delegates, the committee recommend that it be referred to them, in conjuction with the united wisdom of the convention to fix upon a time, when the constitution shall take place. Signed by order and in behalf of the committee, THOMAS LORING, *Chairman.*"

Votes were passed by the town in accordance with the report of the committee.

The representative chosen in May, 1780, was Captain

Charles Cushing. At the same meeting Rev. Daniel Shute was elected delegate to the convention for establishing a new form of government. The town eventually voted for the adoption of the constitution, and on the 4th of September, 1780, the election of state officers took place. The votes for governour in Hingham were 56, of which Hancock had 44, and Bowdoin 12.

On the 9th of October, Capt. Charles Cushing was chosen representative, the first under the constitution.

Our town records at this time, are full of evidence of the active, persevering and liberal efforts of the citizens to carry on to a successful termination, the war in which the colonies were engaged with Great Britain. Town meetings were frequently held, large sums of money raised to be expended in military stores, bounties to soldiers, provisions for their families, and generally for all necessaries to carry on the war.

Committees were appointed to inspect the militia, to procure soldiers, and to keep a vigilant care of the best interests of the people.

The Committee of Correspondence in 1781, were Samuel Norton, Capt. Charles Cushing, Heman Lincoln, Capt. Peter Cushing, and Elisha Cushing, Jr.

The requisitions of the state were generally complied with promptly and cheerfully. In one instance, however, when the General Court "required a quantity of beef or money to be sent in a very short time, and if not complied with, to pay a fine of twenty per cent. ;" the town voted " to comply therewith, provided it be not brought as a precedent in future time."

The Committee of Correspondence, &c. elected in 1782, were Israel Beal, John Fearing and Theophilus Cushing. The same gentlemen were re-elected in 1783.

I have thus presented at length, an account of those

proceedings of the town, from which the feelings of the people may be learned. The individuals who took an active part in their country's cause, merit a conspicuous notice in this history; and it is a source of deep regret to me, that I have not been able to collect a more full and satisfactory account of those noble deeds of individuals which are spread upon no record, and have no memorial except in the imperfect recollections of their aged contemporaries.

It was not by resolutions alone, that the people of Hingham aided the cause of freedom; nor did their meritorious acts consist only in appropriating liberal supplies of money to sustain the liberties of their country; many of them hesitated not to take up arms and to give their lives to a cause to which they were so strongly attached. In a large number of the hard fought battles of the revolution, from the time of the noble display of American valour on Breed's Hill, until that of the brilliant achievements at Yorktown, many of the citizens of Hingham were present sharing the dangers and participating in the honours of the day.* In looking back upon the history of this interesting period, I am aware that some may be found, who hesitated to rally around the banners of their country; some, whose apprehensions of the result of the tremendous conflict, induced them to give but feeble aid to her cause; and perhaps a few who disapproved of the principles, and disregarded the motives which actuated the patriots of those times. But it must be recorded, to their credit, that even the few, made no resistance to the payment of heavy taxes—none, openly, to the power of

* Lt. Joseph Andrews, a brave and promising officer was mortally wounded at the battle of Brandywine. His valour on that occasion attracted much attention. Dulce et decorum est pro patria mori.

public opinion, after the declaration of our independence. Royalists as well as republicans, tories as well as whigs gave of their substance to establish the liberties of their country. The substantial yeomanry of the town, were zealous, determined and persevering ; and the success of their efforts is alike honourable to them and to their posterity.

The delegates chosen by the town to attend the convention for considering the constitution of the United States, proposed by the federal convention, were Gen. Benjamin Lincoln, and Rev. Daniel Shute.

In April, 1788, " the town voted to accept of the Proprietors' ways and of the Proprietors' land not before disposed of, which they at a meeting of theirs, on this present day, made a grant of to the town of Hingham." From the sale of these lands, a considerable fund has been derived, for the support of the poor and schools, as before mentioned.

The first votes given in this town, for a representative to Congress, were, 28 for Fisher Ames, and 1 for Samuel Adams ; and for electors of President and Vice President, 20 for Fisher Ames, 17 for Caleb Davis, and 3 for James Bowdoin.

A sketch of the affairs of this town since 1800 would afford but little interest, and perhaps could not be drawn with perfect impartiality. The political differences or religious disputes which have sprung up during the memory of the living, are better understood already, than they could be from any description of mine. It is proper to mention, that a majority of our citizens approved of the administration of national affairs under *Jefferson* and *Madison*, and disapproved of our state administration during the late war. It is a fact worthy of notice, that all manifested a dispostion to defend their homes and firesides against the common foe, and repaired with alacrity to resist any invasion upon their neighbours.*

Since the war, the affairs of the town have been conducted generally, with unanimity and discretion. The expenditures for the support of public worship, schools, poor, roads and bridges, and for other purposes connected with the general welfare of the community, have sensibly increased, but probably, not in a ratio greater than that of the increase of the number and wealth of the inhabitants.

I here close the civil history of Hingham, and shall next present brief notices of those individuals who have received a public education, and of others, not before noticed, who have been distinguished in public or private life.

* In addition to the three standing companies and one rifle company, already existing, those citizens exempted from military duty, in the last war, formed themselves into three full companies of infantry, and one of artillery—and undoubtedly would have rendered effective service in case of an invasion of our shores.

Graduates at different Universities.*

JOSHUA HOBART, son of Rev. Peter Hobart, first minister of this town, was born in England, and came to this country with his father, in 1635. He was graduated at Harvard University, in 1650, and settled in the ministry at Southhold, Long Island, where he died in March, 1716-7, aged 89 years.

JEREMIAH HOBART, son of Rev. Peter Hobart, was born in England, and accompanied his father's family to this country, in 1635. He was graduated at Harvard University, in 1650. He settled in the ministry, first at

* Unless otherwise mentioned, they were all natives of Hingham.

Topsfield, Massachusetts, and then removed to Hempstead, Long Island, " and afterwards removed from Hempstead (by reason of numbers turning quakers, and many others being so irreligious that they would do nothing towards the support of the ministry)"* and settled at Haddam, Connecticut, November 14, 1700. He died at Haddam, March, 1717, aged 87 years.

GERSHOM HOBART, son of Rev. Peter Hobart, was born in December, 1645, and graduated at Harvard University, in 1667. He was settled as a minister at Groton, Massachusetts, November 26, 1679. From what I can learn of his situation at Groton, he appears not to have been fortunate in conciliating the esteem of the people of his charge. Previously to his settlement, the town had made him liberal grants of land, on the condition that he settled there in the ministry ; and after his settlement, a salary adequate to his maintenance was granted him. In 1685,† some new arrangement was made respecting his salary, which he appears to have disliked, and he expressed himself in a manner which excited the feelings of the people against him. In December, 1685, the inhabitants in town meeting, voted, unanimously, " that Mr. Gershom Hobart has set himself at liberty from the said town, as to any engagement from him to them as their minister, and has freed the town from any engagement to himself, by refusing and slighting what the town offered him for his salary." In consequence of this disagreement, Mr. Hobart relinquished his labours as a minister, and it does not appear that any reconciliation was effected, although the town made several other propositions to him, which he de-

* Life of Brainerd by Rev. J. Edwards.
† Groton Town Records.

clined accepting. The date of his final dismission cannot be ascertained. He died Dec. 19th, 1707, aged 62 years.

JAPHETH HOBART, son of Rev. Peter Hobart, was born in April, 1647, and graduated at Harvard University in 1667. Before the time for taking his second degree, he went to England in the capacity of surgeon of a ship, with a design to go from thence to the East Indies, but never was heard of afterwards.*

NEHEMIAH HOBART, the fifth son of Rev. Peter Hobart, who received a liberal education, was born November 21, 1648, and graduated at Harvard University, in 1667. He was ordained pastor of the church at Newton, Mass. Dec. 23, 1674. He was a fellow of Harvard University from 1707 to 1712. He died in August of the latter year. " In him (it is said,) shone the scholar, the gentleman and the christian." The following is a copy of an epitaph on his tomb-stone : " Hoc tumulo depositae sunt reliquiae reverendi et perdocti D. D. Nehemiae Hobart, Collegii Harvardini, socii lectissimi, ecclesiae Neotoniensis per annos quadraginta pastoris fidelissimi—et vigilantissimi, singulare gravitate, humilitate aeque ac pietate et doctrina—a doctis et piis eximia veneratione et amore recolendi:" et cet. of which I suppose the substance in our own tongue will be the most acceptable to some readers. It is as follows, viz : " Within this tomb are deposited the remains of the reverend and very learned doctor of divinity Nehemiah Hobart, a very excellent fellow of Harvard College, and faithful and vigilant pastor of the church at Newton, during forty years ;—distinguished for gravity and humility and also for piety and learning ; and held by the pious and learned in peculiar veneration and esteem."

* Life of Brainerd.

JEREMIAH CUSHING, son of Daniel Cushing, Esq. was born July 3, 1654, and graduated at Harvard University, in 1676. He received an invitation to settle in the ministry at Haverhill, in 1682, which he declined accepting. He was afterwards invited to become the pastor of the church in Scituate, and was ordained over it, May 27,1691.

JEDIDIAH ANDREWS, son of Capt. Thomas Andrews, was born July 7, 1674, graduated at Harvard University in 1695 and afterwards settled in the ministry at Philadelphia.

DANIEL LEWIS, son of John Lewis, was born September 29, 1685, and graduated at Harvard University, in 1707. A ter he was graduated, he taught the grammar school in Hingham, until 1712, when he was invited to settle in the ministry at Pembroke. He accepted the invitation and was ordained December 3, 1712.

NEHEMIAH HOBART, son of David Hobart, and grandson of Rev. Peter Hobart, was born April 27, 1697, graduated at Harvard University, in 1714, and was ordained pastor of the second church in Hingham, now Cohasset, December 13, 1721. He died May 31, 1740.

SAMUEL THAXTER, son of Col. Samuel Thaxter, was born October 8, 1695, and graduated at Harvard University, in 1714. He died in Hingham December 4, 1732.

JOB CUSHING, son of Matthew Cushing, was born July 19, 1694, and graduated at Harvard University, in 1714. He was the first minister of Shrewsbury, Mass. and was ordained December 4, 1723. He died August 6, 1760.

ADAM CUSHING, son of Theophilus Cushing, was born

January 1, 1692-3, and graduated at Harvard University, in 1714.

CORNELIUS NYE, for many years a teacher of a school in Hingham, was graduated at Harvard University, in 1718. He died in 1749, aged 52.

ISAAC LINCOLN, son of David Lincoln, was born January 18, 1701-2, and graduated at Harvard University, in 1722. He studied divinity, but relinquished the profession, and taught a school in Hingham for a great number of years. He died April 19, 1760.

ISAIAH LEWIS, son of John Lewis, was born June 10, 1703, graduated at Harvard University, in 1723, and settled in the ministry at Eastham, now Wellfleet. He died October 3, 1786.

NOAH HOBART, son of David, and brother of Rev. Nehemiah Hobart, of Cohasset, was born January 2, 1705, and graduated at Harvard University, in 1724. He was settled as a minister at Fairfield, Conn. February 7, 1732. A few years after his settlement, a number of persons in Fairfield County, adopted the episcopalian worship, and separated themselves from the congregational churches. The episcopal missionaries represented the ministers of the country as not the true ministers of Christ. In consequence of these representations, Mr. Hobart preached a sermon in 1746, to vindicate the validity of presbyterian ordination; to which Mr. Wetmore of North Haven replied. This commenced a controversy in which Mr. Hobart had for his opponents, Dr. Johnson, Mr. Wetmore, Mr. Beach and Mr. Caner. "He contended, that the inhabitants of the American plantations were not obliged by any laws of God or man to conform to the prelatic church, as established in the south part of Great Britain, that it was not prudent to embrace the episcopal communion, and that it was not lawful for members of the New England churches to separate from them and produce a schism. He also animadverted upon the conduct of the society for propagating the gospel in foreign parts, and upon the misrepresentations of its missionaries. This controversy lasted a number of years. Mr. Hobart died December 6, 1773, in the sixty eighth year of his age, and the forty first of his ministry. In his life he exhibited the virtues, and in his death the resignation and peace of the Christian. Not long before his departure from the world, as some one remarked to him, that he was going to receive his reward, he replied, " I am going, I trust, to receive the mercy of God through Jesus Christ."

" Mr. Hobart had few equals in this country for acuteness of genius and learning. A sound judgment, a retentive memory, and an uncommonly social and communicative temper, joined to a knowledge of books, and an extensive acquaintance with most branches of science, especially with history and divinity, which were his favourite studies, rendered his conversation very interesting and useful. In the public offices of religion he acquitted himself with graceful dignity, and with a solemnity, which indicated a deep impression of the majesty of that Being, in whose presence he appeared. In his preaching he addressed himself to the understanding rather than to the imagination and passions, inculcating the great doctrines of regeneration, of repentance towards God, and faith in Jesus Christ, and pressing with earnestness upon his hearers the necessity of that holiness, without which no man will be admitted to heaven."—*Allen's Bio. Dic.*

THOMAS GILL, was born October 12, 1707, and graduated at Harvard University, in 1725. He resided in Hingham, and was a delegate to the General Court in 1742, 1743 and 1744. He died March 19, 1761.

JEREMIAH CHUBBUCK, was born March 31, 1704, and graduated at Harvard University in 1725. He resided for some time in Hingham, and afterwards removed, but to what place, is unknown.

JOSEPH LEWIS, son of Joseph Lewis, was born December 1, 1705, and graduated at Harvard University, in 1725. After he had completed his education, he resided in Boston, where he was a merchant. He afterwards removed to Hingham, and taught a school for a considerable number of years. He died January 14, 1786.

THOMAS LEWIS, brother of the preceding, was born September 30, 1707, and graduated at Harvard University, in 1728. He studied divinity and preached occasionally. He abandoned the profession, and died in Hingham, April 4, 1787.

EZEKIEL HERSEY, son of James Hersey, was born September 21, 1709, and graduated at Harvard University, in 1728. He settled in his native town as a physician. He became eminent in his profession. In the controversy between the colonies and the mother country, he espoused the cause of the former, and his opinions had a most favourable effect on the community in which he lived. His charities were extensive, as his means were adequate to do much good. He was among the benefactors of Harvard University. In his will, executed November 29, 1770, he directed his executrix to pay to the corporation of that University, £1000, "the interest thereof to be by them appropriated towards the support of a professor of anatomy and physic." His widow gave the same sum for the same purpose. A professorship was established on this foundation, entitled the Hersey professorship of anatomy and surgery. Dr. Hersey died December 9, 1770.

James Lewis, son of Joseph Lewis, was born September 9, 1712, and graduated at Harvard University in 1731. He removed to Marshfield, where he taught a school, and died in that town.

Thomas Marsh was graduated at Harvard University, in 1731. He was a Tutor of the University from 1741 to 1766, and a Fellow from 1755 to 1766. He died at Watertown, during the Revolutionary War.

Benjamin Pratt, son of Aaron Pratt, was born March 13, 1710-11, in that part of Hingham now included within the limits of Cohasset. He was graduated at Harvard University, in 1737. He entered that seminary at an advanced standing, in the junior class, and was distinguished for the extent of his acquirements, and the maturity of his judgment. His distinguished talents and the strong and powerful motives of an ambitious mind, pointed to the course which he finally pursued. He read law with Auchmuty or Gridley, or both, and commenced business in Boston. He was a man preeminently intellectual, and possesed those strong and decided traits of character which were calculated to render him not only conspicuous at the bar, but made his course sure and easy to the highest political distinctions. For several years, he was one of the representatives of Boston in the legislature, and was a constant, fearless, and independent lover of freedom ; and never hesitated to support what he thought was just, wise and expedient. He was an independent whig. His learning and eloquence gained him the intimate friendship of governour Pownal, and in a state of strong political excitement, by his attentions to the governour, he incurred the jealousy of the people, and he was left out of the list of representatives. Obstinate prejudices frequently arise out of trifling and even from honourable transactions ; yet so powerful is their force, that the most shining ornaments of the political world are sometimes distrusted and neglected. Pratt possessed all the pride of a New England man. But the land of his nativity was not destined to be the scene of his usefulness, or to reap the glorious reward of cherishing an honourable ambition to attain the well earned reputation of an elegant scholar and a profound lawyer. By the influence of Pownal, he was appointed Chief Justice of the Supreme Court of New York. On the occasion of his separation from the bar of Suffolk, the members sent him a valedictory address, which affectionately spoke of his worth. His answer was a classical composition, full of dignity and feeling.

Many of the people of Boston thought him morose, distant and haughty ; but they did not fully understand him. To the few for whom he felt a high respect for their worth and intelligence, he was courteous and communicative. His talents were never questioned by any. It is not improbable that his early misfortune, the loss of a limb, gave a sober cast to his character. The character of Pratt's eloquence and of his poetry, prove that he reasoned much upon the nature of man, and upon the wisdom and design of God in making him what he is. He must have been a man of great research and learning, for he had made such an extensive collection of rare documents, relating to the events of this country, that he contemplated writing a history of New England ; but he died too soon to accomplish it. This was deeply regretted by all who knew how well qualified he was for such a task. The public on this account alone, lost much by his death, for his style was far superior to that of any man of his time. His models were classical, and his manner free from the gravity then prevalent among American writers. He frequently wrote poetry which was published in the newspapers and magazines of the day. A canto on death, which is traced to him, proves that he had taste and fancy.

Pratt's domestic character was amiable ; in conversation he was attractive and pleasing ; nor was he deficient in urbanity of manners. He married a daughter of Judge Auchmuty ; she is said to have been an accomplished woman, and to have been equally competent to appreciate his virtues and intellect.

Chief Justice Pratt contemplated a return to New-England, to spend the close of life, but this agreeable anticipation was never realized. He died at New York, January 5, 1763. "Death is not charmed by eloquence, nor warded off by virtues ; the monarch of worlds loves to point his dart near the throne of Omnipotence, and to send those who bear the brightest image of their Maker to mingle with kindred spirits."—*Knapp's Sketches, Anthology and Am. Bio. Dic.*

MATTHEW CUSHING, was graduated, at Harvard University, in 1739. He afterwards taught a school at Plymouth, and at Charlestown, Massachusetts. Thence he removed to New York, where he died.

SAMUEL GAY, son of Ebenezer Gay, D. D. the third minister of Hingham, was born January 15, 1720, and graduated at Harvard University, in 1740. He studied medicine, and went to England to obtain professional information, where he died, before the completion of his studies.

JOHN THAXTER, son of John Thaxter, was born November 22, 1721, and graduated at Harvard University, in 1741. He settled in his native town, and was a respectable, intelligent and wealthy farmer. He was a representative to the General Court, in 1772. He died October 6, 1802.

SAMUEL THAXTER, son of Samuel Thaxter, was born November, 15, 1723, and graduated at Harvard University, in 1743. He was an officer in the war between the English, and the French and Indians, and was present, at the massacre after the capitulation of Fort William Henry, in 1757, from which he fortunately escaped. In the last part of his life he lived in Bridgewater, where he died August 6, 1771.

SAMUEL FRENCH was graduated at Harvard University, in 1748, and studied divinity. He is represented as an excellent scholar and an amiable man. He died May 21, 1752, in the 23d year of his age.

BELA LINCOLN, son of Hon. Benjamin Lincoln, and a brother of General Benjamin Lincoln of the Revolutionary Army, was born in March, 1733-4. He was graduated at Harvard University, in 1754. He studied the profession of medicine, and settled in his native town. After he had practiced for a considerable time, he visited Europe for the purpose of obtaining professional information ; and received the degree of Doctor of Medicine, from the University of Aberdeen. His constitution was feeble, but his intellectual powers were vigorous and strong. He took an active part in the cause of his country during the controversies that preceded the Revolution ; but did not live till the time of the declaration of our independence, nor to participate either in the toils and dangers which were subsequently endured by the friends of civil liberty, or in the rich blessings which its establishment produced. He died July 13, 1773.

JOSEPH THAXTER, son of Dea. Joseph Thaxter, was was born April 23, 1744, and graduated at Harvard University, in 1768. After he was graduated, he spent considerable time in his native town, as a teacher of a public school. When hostilities commenced between this country and Great Britain, in 1775, he was preaching as a candidate for the ministry at Westford, and on the advance of the British troops towards Lexington, he hastened to Concord on horseback, armed with a brace of pistols, and was among those who received the fire of the enemy at Concord Bridge. He was afterwards appointed a chaplain to the army and was attached to Prescott's regiment, at the time of the battle at Breed's Hill. During the war, he was chosen by his fellow citizens at Hingham, to represent them in the General Court, which situation he resigned, to discharge more active and important duties in the army. After the acknowledgement of our independence, he settled in the ministry at Edgartown, where he lived for a great length of time in the discharge of his duty as a faithful, zealous and useful divine. He participated in the ceremonies of the 17th of June, 1825, at the laying of the corner stone of the Bunker Hill Monument. He was at that time the only surviving chaplain of the revolutionary army. Few who were present, will forget the fervent and devotional prayer which this venerable patriot uttered on that occasion, or the patriarchal appearance of that early, zealous and persevering advocate of civil and religious liberty. He died, July 18, 1827.

JOSHUA BARKER, son of Capt. Francis Barker, was born March 24, 1753, and graduated at Harvard University, in 1772. He studied medicine with the late Dr. Danforth of Boston. A gentleman who was intimately acquainted with Dr. Barker, thus describes his character :

" With a mind naturally active and capable of improvement, he had enjoyed the advantages of a liberal education, upon which he continued through life to improve by study. Having chosen for his profession the practice of physic, after a regular course of preparatory study, he settled as a physician in his native town, where he continued to practice with reputation and success, until he was taken off from his active and useful labors by an attack on the nervous system, which, after a gradual and distressing decay of near eleven months, terminated in dissolution. As a physician, his attention to the sick was always prompt, kind and impartial, and administered with the same readiness to the rich and poor. In the domestic and social relations, and in his character as a member of civil society, few men were more justly esteemed and respected, than Dr. Barker. An easy politeness, refined taste, cheerful hospitality, and intellectual conversation made his house a pleasant resort to his friends and acquaintances, and by his attentive notice of strangers who visited the town, he was an honour to the place in which he lived.

In friendship, he was warm and affectionate, yet steady and faithful. In his dealings he was regular, methodical, punctual and conscientiously upright. As a citizen, a firm friend to liberty, order and peace, he was a friend to all the institutions of his country which have the promotion of these for their object, whether civil, religious, or literary ; and was always ready by his example, his influence, his exertions, and the contribution of his property, to promote them."

Dr. Barker was in the habit of corresponding with many distinguished gentlemen of his profession, and enjoyed their esteem and regard. He took a deep interest in the unfortunate IBBEKIN, a German who resided for some time in this town, and who amused himself with visionary attempts to fly like a bird ! His experiments proving unsuccessful, he shot himself in a " paroxysm of despair." Some account of Ibbekin may be found in the appendix, in a letter from Dr. Waterhouse to Dr. Barker.

Dr. Barker died April 2, 1800, as deeply lamented in death, as he had been amiable, useful and deserving in life.

LEVI LINCOLN. To the character of this distinguished lawyer and civilian, I have no expectation of doing justice, in the slight sketch which I am obliged to present of it. He was one of eleven children of Mr. Enoch Lincoln, an intelligent and substantial farmer in Hingham, who had rendered his fellow citizens considerable services during the Revolution, having been frequently on important committees, and a representative to the General Court. Not intending to grant to one of his children advantages, which he was unable to offer to all ; his son Levi was placed at the usual age as an apprentice to an Iron Smith.* He soon exhibited indications of talent, and a love of literary pursuits which attracted the attention of his friends and acquaintances. He devoted much of his time to reading, and to the study of the Latin and Greek languages, in which he received considerable assistance from Mr. Joseph Lewis, who taught a grammar school in this place for many years, and also from Dr. Gay, who took a deep interest in his welfare. His love of books soon created a disrelish for the occupation in which he was engaged. They were his companions by day and by night. He generally appeared as if engaged in deep thought, and by some was considered reserved and distant in his manners. There was a degree of seriousness in his deportment, and propriety in his conduct, which procured for him the esteem of the virtuous and the good. His love of literature increased with his years, until, at length, his friends and acquaintances expressed a general desire that he should receive the advantages of a collegiate education. He accordingly abandoned his trade, and after a few months preparation, he entered Harvard University, at the age of 19, and was graduated at that seminary, in 1772. After he was graduated, he read law with HAWLEY, and commenced the practice of his profession, at Worcester, in 1775. He soon became distinguished, and for more than twenty years, was at the head of his profession in that county.

He was appointed Clerk of the Court of Common Pleas, in 1775, and in the succeeding year, Judge of Probate for the County of Worcester. In 1781, he was elected a delegate to Congress under the Confederation; in 1787, he was re-appointed a delegate, but declined the office. In 1797, he was a senator from Worcester Coun-

* See page 90.

ty; and in 1800, was chosen to represent that district in Congress. He took his seat, March 4, 1801, and the next day was appointed by President Jefferson, Attorney General of the United States. He resigned in 1805. He discharged the duties of Secretary of State under Mr. Jefferson, until Mr. Madison reached Washington. In 1807, he was elected Lieutenant Governour of Massachusetts, and re-elected in 1808, when, in consequence of Governour Sullivan's death, the administration devolved on Mr. Lincoln. In 1810, he was elected a member of the Executive Council of this Commonwealth, and in 1811, he was appointed an Associate Justice of the Supreme Court of the United States, which office he declined, and soon after retired to private life.

The number of important offices which Mr. Lincoln filled give some indication of the estimation in which his talents were held by the people, and by some of the most distinguished statesmen of the country. He was learned in his profession, and in his addresses to a jury, eloquent and sometimes irresistible. As a statesman, he was fearless and independent, and obtained respect by his energy and decision of character, and not by the practice of any arts to secure popular favour and public admiration.

The following remark on the character of Mr. Lincoln, appeared in the Worcester Spy a few days after his decease, which took place April 14, 1820.

"The death of Lieutenant Governour LINCOLN is an event calulated to excite the most interesting considerations in the minds of those engaged in tracing the origin and progress of our laws and judicial institutions.

"Deservedly placed at the head of his profession in this county, for many years, it is a proper subject of inquiry, especially by the juniors of his profession, how was this ascendency acquired, and so long maintained?

"With perhaps but one or two exceptions, we have now followed to the tomb the last of that illustrious band of Statesmen and Lawyers, who laid the foundation of that admirable system of government and laws, which for forty years has afforded security, and dispensed blessings to our Commonwealth. Their works form for them, collectively, a monument durable as our liberties; but, without the aid of some faithful biographer, what will posterity know of them individually? Our Law Reports have, indeed, "erected a frail memorial" for those who have been accidentally named in them—but those whose plastick hands formed and matured the majestic fabric of our laws and liberties, who gave the first practical construction to our Constitution, will soon be remembered no more.—While we are protected and comforted by its shade, it certainly would be an instructive as well as curious employment to trace from the acorn the gradual developement and growth of the majestic oak, under whose branches we sit. The few surviving contemporaries of Cushing, Dana, Parsons, the Strongs, Sewall, Sullivan, Sedgwick, Lincoln and their companions, owe it not only to posterity, but to the greater part of the present generation to place upon record the history of their lives, particularly those instructive and interesting anecdotes that connect them with the great history of the country. Few of our lawyers and divines are acquainted with the fact that the arbitrary encroachments of the Royalist clergymen in the year 1776, were first successfully resisted here, and that too by Mr. LINCOLN—that it probably was his exertions that first defined and settled the often conflicting interests of Minister, Church, and Parish. How few of our rising politicians have been taught that the first practical comment on the introductory clause of the Bill of Rights, was first given by a Worcester jury

That it was here first shown, by the irresistible eloquence of LINCOLN, that 'all men were in truth *born free and equal*,' and that a court sitting under the authority of our Constitution, *could not* admit as a justification for an assault, the principle of *Master* and *Slave* :—That it was the memorable verdict obtained upon this trial, which first broke the fetters of negro slavery in Massachusetts, and let the oppressed free. This deed of Judge LINCOLN, even if it stood alone, ought to consecrate his memory with every freeman."

At the decease of Mr. Lincoln, the Bar of the County of Worcester adopted resolutions expressive of their veneration of his distinguished learning and eloquence, and of respect for his memory.

MARTIN LEAVITT, son of Elisha Leavitt, was born March 20, 1755, and graduated at Harvard University, in 1773; he was a physician and practised a few years. He died, November 27, 1785.

THOMAS LORING, son of Thomas Loring, was graduated at Harvard University, in 1774; he is now a merchant in Hingham.

JOHN THAXTER, son of Col. John Thaxter, was born July 5, 1755, and graduated at Harvard University, in 1774; he read law in the office of the late President Adams, at Braintree, and in 1776, was appointed Deputy Secretary to Congress. Afterwards, in the absence of Mr. Thomson, he performed the duties of Secretary with honour and fidelity. In this station, his prudence, attention and propriety of conduct gained the friendship of *many* and the esteem of *all* the members of Congress, and introduced him to the particular notice of President Laurens. In

1779, when Mr. Adams was appointed Minister Plenipotentiary to make a Treaty of Peace, and also a Treaty of Commerce, with Great Britain, Mr. Thaxter accompanied him to Europe, in the character of Private Secretary. With Mr. Adams he resided in France and Holland; and while his taste for literature rendered him an agreeable companion, his integrity and perfect fidelity in the duties of his station, claimed and received the utmost confidence of that patriotic statesman. Peace being confirmed in 1783, the Commissioners sent him to America, with the charge of presenting the Definitive Treaty to Congress; he was received with attention and respect.

In 1784, he commenced the practice of law at Haverhill, Massachusetts, where he died, July 5, 1791. A gentleman who knew him thus speaks of his character:

" As a *Lawyer*, Mr. Thaxter was eminently respected for those qualifications, the want of which in some of the profession, has brought a degree of odium upon the whole ' Order.' A nervous system, too delicate by nature to withstand the imperious taunts of over-bearing arrogance, and still more debilitated by disease, disappointed the expectations which his strong manly style of sentiment had created, and unhappily rendered him less useful, as an advocate at the Bar, than as a Counsellor in his Chamber. But he was rich in the less glaring virtues; honour, integrity, fidelity, and love of peace. These gained him the esteem and confidence of all.

" As a *Magistrate* he was revered—and the blessing of the Peace-maker was upon him.

" As a *Man*, he possessed those amiable accomplishments which meliorate and adorn, together with those more austere virtues, which correct and dignify human nature. In his nearest connections, he was fervent and affectionate. In his friendships, warm, sincere, and confidential. In his family he was frugal, that, by the exercises of benevolence, he might gratify that disposition of mind, which was his greatest source of happiness. While the rich mourn him as the faithful guardian of their property, the poor bless his memory, as that of a friend.

" His religion was pure—and he evinced his attachment to it by his punctual attendance on its rites and duties. Its most happy effects were displayed in his latest hours; conscious of intentional rectitude, and conscious of his rapid dissolution, his only anxiety was for his wife and daughter ; commending them to the care of his friends, and to the protection of the Almighty, his last moments were calm and composed. *The End of that Man was Peace.*"

PETER HOBART, son of Dea. Peter Hobart, was born July 31, 1750, and graduated at Harvard University, in 1775 ; he settled in Hanover, Massachusetts, as a physician, where he died.

DANIEL SHUTE, son of Daniel Shute, D. D. was graduated at Harvard University, in 1775 ; and settled in his native town, as a physician, where he now resides.

BENJAMIN LINCOLN, son of Gen. Benjamin Lincoln, was born November 1, 1756, and graduated at Harvard University, in 1777. He is said to have been distinguished in a class which contained a Bentley, a Freeman, a Dawes, and a King. He read law in the office of the late Lieut. Gov. Lincoln, at Worcester, and commenced the practice of his profession in Boston ; he there acquired an honourable reputation, but his flattering hopes of future distinction were destroyed by his death, in 1788.

THEODORE LINCOLN, brother of the preceding, was graduated at Harvard University, in 1785; he now resides in Dennysville, Maine.

JOHN ANDREWS, D. D. son of Joseph Andrews, was graduated at Harvard University, in 1786; he studied divinity, and was settled in the ministry at Newburyport, in 1788.

HENRY LINCOLN, son of William Lincoln, was graduated at Harvard University, in 1786; studied divinity, and was settled in the ministry at Falmouth, Barnstable County, Massachusetts, in 1790. The connexion between Mr. Lincoln and the society was dissolved, by mutual consent, in 1823. He now resides at Nantucket.

ABNER LINCOLN, son of Nathan Lincoln, was born July 17, 1766, and graduated at Harvard University, in 1788. He was the first Preceptor of Derby Academy, and was appointed by the request of Mrs. Derby. He remained in this office for several years; and many of his pupils yet recollect with grateful feelings, the amiable qualities, the happy faculty of teaching, and the perseverance with which he devoted himself to the promotion of their good. The connexion of teacher and pupil is often productive of agreeable associations in after life, and frequently a tie of friendship is formed between them, which is separated only by death. Mr. Lincoln could number many among his numerous pupils, who retained a strong feeling of personal regard for him, and from whom he received the most friendly memorials of their esteem.

Mr. Lincoln was a magistrate of the county of Plymouth, and frequently presided at the trial of causes.

He was distinguished for general intelligence, an easy and agreeable address, and a practical knowledge of mankind. He died, June 10, 1826.

Levi Lincoln, son of Levi Lincoln, was graduated at Harvard University, in 1789. He studied medicine and settled in his native town, where he now resides.

Isaiah Cushing, son of Maj. Isaiah Cushing, was born February 20, 1777, and graduated at Harvard University, in 1798. He studied medicine, and settled in Maine. He died a few years since.

Perez Lincoln, son of David Lincoln, was born January 21, 1777, and graduated at Harvard University, in 1798. He studied divinity with the late Dr. Barnes, of Scituate ; and was settled in the ministry at Gloucester, Massachusetts, August 8, 1805. He was esteemed a talented, and promising divine ; but his constitution was feeble, and the people of his charge enjoyed the benefit of his ministerial labours for only a few years. He died, June 13, 1811.

Robert Thaxter, son of Dr. Thomas Thaxter, was graduated at Harvard University, in 1798 ; and is now a physician at Dorchester, Massachusetts.

Caleb Rice, son of Col. Nathan Rice, was graduated at Harvard University, in 1803. He now resides in Hingham.

Andrews Norton, son of Samuel Norton, Esq. was graduated at Harvard University, in 1804. He is the present Professor of Sacred Literature, in that Seminary.

ABNER LORING, son of Peter Loring, was born July 21, 1786, and graduated at Harvard University, in 1807. He read law in the office of Hon. Ebenezer Gay ; and commenced the practice of his profession at Dorchester, Massachusetts. Mr. Loring was well read in his profession, devoted to business, and possessed of an unexceptionable character for fairness and integrity. He promised to become an ornament to his profession. But the anticipations of friendship are not always realized ; and the hopes of the public are frequently disappointed. Mr. Loring died, deeply lamented, July 18, 1814.

DANIEL SHUTE, son of Daniel Shute, M. D. was graduated at Harvard University, in 1812 ; and is now a physician in Hingham.

HENRY WARE, Jr. was graduated at Harvard University, in 1812, and is now the Pastor of the Second Congregational Church, in Boston.

JEROME LORING, son of Jonathan Loring, was graduated at Brown University, in 1813. He now resides in Delaware.

JOHN WARE, son of Henry Ware, D. D. was graduated at Harvard University, in 1813 ; and is now a physician in Boston.

JOHN THAXTER, son of Quincy Thaxter, was born November 4, 1793, and graduated at Harvard University, in 1814. He read law in the office of Hon. Ebenezer Gay, at Hingham, and settled in Scituate, where he died, in 1824.

WILLIAM WARE, son of Henry Ware, D. D. was graduated at Harvard University, in 1816, and is now pastor of a Unitarian Church in the City of New York.

HENRY HERSEY, son of Capt. Laban Hersey, was graduated at Brown University, in 1820; and is now settled in the ministry at Barnstable, Massachusetts.

CALVIN LINCOLN, Jr. was graduated at Harvard University, in 1820; and is now settled in the ministry at Fitchburg, Massachusetts. He was ordained, June 30, 1824.

JACOB HERSEY LOUD, son of Thomas Loud, Esq., was graduated at Brown University, in 1822; and is now an Attorney at Law, in Plymouth, Massachusetts.

SOLOMON LINCOLN, Jr. was graduated at Brown University, in 1822; and is now an Attorney at Law, in Hingham.

WILLIAM ALEXANDER GORDON, son of Dr. William Gordon, of Hingham, is a native of Newburyport; was graduated at Harvard University, in 1826; and is now a medical student in Hingham.

UNDERGRADUATES.

At Harvard University, JAMES HUMPHREY WILDER, son of Abiel Wilder.
At Brown University, CHARLES GORDON, son of Doct. William Gordon; and GEORGE BRONSON, son of the late Capt. S. Bronson.

CLERGYMEN OF HINGHAM.

Rev. JOSEPH RICHARDSON, a native of Billerica, and a graduate of Dartmouth College, in 1802.

Rev. NICHOLAS BOWES WHITNEY, a native of Shirley, and a graduate of Harvard University, in 1793.

Rev. CHARLES BROOKS, a native of Medford, and a graduate of Harvard University, in 1816.

COUNSELLOR AT LAW.

Hon. EBENEZER GAY, a graduate of Harvard University, in 1789.

ATTORNEY AT LAW.

SOLOMON LINCOLN, Jr. a graduate of Brown University, in 1822.

PRACTISING PHYSICIANS.

WILLIAM GORDON.

DANIEL SHUTE, Jr. Harvard University, 1812.

ROBERT T. P. FISKE, Harvard University, 1818.

Additional Biographical Notices.

The following notices relate to individuals who did not enjoy the advantages of a collegiate education.

DANIEL CUSHING, the third Town Clerk of Hingham, and who rendered important services to the town, in that office, for more than thirty years, merits a more extended notice than it is practicable to give in this work. He was a son of Matthew Cushing, and was born in Hingham, England, in 1619. He accompanied his father's family to this country in 1638, and settled in Hingham. I find in the old records, that he was frequently chosen by the inhabitants to transact their most important business, on committees, as an assessor, &c. He was a magistrate; and as such, was frequently called upon to settle disputes among the citizens and to preside at the trial of causes. He often held courts for the trial of the Indians and others who had violated the laws of the country; and from the evidence I have of his mode of procedure, I should think him unusually correct and intelligent for the time in which he lived. Among his papers, there are preserved perfect accounts of the trial of actions for slander, libel, assault, trespasses, &c., which indicate that he was a judicious and independent magistrate. Mr. Cushing was elected to the office of Town Clerk, in 1669, and retained the office until his decease. The records during his term of office, are kept with great care and neatness; and can be properly valued only by those who have had occasion to become acquainted with the early records of our old settlements.

The invaluable services which Mr. Cushing rendered the public, do not appear to have been properly appreciated by his fellow citizens; indeed, there is a tradition, that many valuable papers relating to the affairs of the town, which he had prepared, are now lost, in consequence of the refusal of the town to make him a proper and reasonable compensation for them.

Mr. Cushing was a delegate to the General Court, in 1680, and 1682, and was chosen in 1689, a delegate to the council of safety, but declined the office.

Many of the papers which Mr. Cushing prepared relating to the early history of Hingham, are yet preserved. His Diary contains notes of some transactions and events, which are to be found in no other record; but much of it is imperfect, and a considerable portion of it is lost. Mr. Cushing died December 3, 1700.

ABNER HERSEY, son of James Hersey, and a brother of Dr. Ezekiel Hersey of this town, was an eminent physician at Barnstable, Massachusetts. He bequeathed to Harvard University £500 towards the establishment of a professorship of the theory and practice of physic. The first professor in this department was Dr. Waterhouse. Dr. Hersey also bequeathed about £500, the interest of which he directed to be applied annually to the purchase of religious publications, which should be distributed in all the towns on Cape Cod. He directed what books should be selected for a hundred years; after the expiration of which time, the ministers and deacons of the several towns, to whose care his donation was entrusted, were authorized to select any religious books at their pleasure, excepting on every fourth year, when the books which he designated, among which were some of Doddridge's works, were to be distributed forever. This singular bequest proved to be of much less value than Dr. Hersey had anticipated; he seems not to have considered the inconvenience of carrying it into execution, nor to have calculated that the increasing population of a whole county, could derive but little benefit from his bequest. In consequence of the trifling advantages accruing to the several towns mentioned, from this fund, they made an arrangement, a few years since, for its distribution among the churches of Barnstable County in such a manner that it would be an essential benefit to all : this arrangement was made with the consent of the heirs of Dr. Hersey.—*Allen's Bio. Dic.*

BENJAMIN LINCOLN.—General Benjamin Lincoln of the army of the revolution, was a son of Hon. Benjamin Lincoln,* of Hingham, and was born January 24, 1732-3.† The only advantages of early education which he enjoyed were those afforded by our public schools, and his occupation till he was more than forty years of age, was that of a farmer. Previously to the revolution he had become an active and influential citizen. He was elected town clerk of Hingham, in 1757 ; he was generally placed on all important committees chosen by the town to consider the subjects of the controversy between the Colonies and Great Britain ; he represented Hingham in the General Court, in 1772, 1773, and 1774, and, as mentioned in the sketches of the civil history of the town, he was chosen to attend the Provincial Congress at Concord, Cambridge, and Watertown. He had been, previously to this date, commissioned as a magistrate. In the year 1775, he sustained the office of lieutenant colonel of militia, and was one of the secretaries of the Provincial Congress. In

---

* See note to page 93.
† In Thacher's Military Journal, it is erroneously stated that Gen. Lincoln was born "January 23d, O. S. 1733." From Hingham town records of births, &c., as above.

1776, he was appointed by the council of Massachusetts a brigadier, and soon after a major general, and he applied himself assiduously to training and preparing the militia for actual service.

In October, 1776, he marched with a body of militia, and joined the main army at New York. The commander in chief, from a knowledge of his character and merit, recommended him to Congress as an excellent officer, and in February following, he was created a major general on the continental establishment. For several months he commanded a detachment of the main army under General Washington, and was placed in situations requiring the exercise of the utmost vigilance and caution, as well as firmness and courage. Having the command of about five hundred men in an exposed situation near Bound Brook, through the neglect of the patroles, a large body of the enemy approached undiscovered within two hundred yards of his quarters ; the General had scarcely time to mount and leave the house before it was surrounded. He led off his troops however, and made good his retreat, with the loss of about sixty men killed and wounded. One of his aids with the General's baggage and papers fell into the hands of the enemy, as did also three pieces of artillery. In July, 1777, he was selected by Washington to join the northern army under the command of General Gates, to oppose the advance of Burgoyne. He took his station at Manchester, in Vermont, to receive and form the New England militia as they arrived, and to order their march to the rear of the British army. He detached Colonel Brown with five hundred men, on the 13th of September, to the landing at lake George, where he succeeded in surprising the enemy, and took two hundred batteaux, several gunboats and an armed sloop ; liberated one hundred American prisoners, and captured two hundred and ninety-three of the enemy, with the loss of only three killed and five wounded. This enterprize contributed essentially to the glorious event which followed. Having detached two other parties to the enemy's posts at Mount Independence and Skenesborough, General Lincoln united his remaining force with the army under General Gates, and was the second in command. During the sanguinary conflict on the 7th of October, General Lincoln commanded within the lines, and at one o'clock the next morning, he marched with his division to the relief of the troops that had been engaged, and to occupy the battle ground, the enemy having retreated. While on this duty, he rode forward some distance to reconnoitre, and to order some disposition of his own troops, when a party of the enemy made an unexpected movement, and he approached within musket shot before he discovered his mistake. A volley of musketry was discharged at him and his aids, and he received a wound by which the bones of his leg were badly fractured, and he was obliged to be carried off the field. The wound was a formidable one, and the loss of his limb was for some time apprehended. It became necessary to remove a considerable portion of the main bone before he was removed to Hingham, and under the most painful operation, he is said to have exhibited uncommon firmness and patience; he did not entirely recover from this wound for several years, and it occasioned lameness during the remainder of his life. General Lincoln afforded very important assistance in the capture of Burgoyne, though it was his unfortunate lot, while in active duty, to be disabled before he could participate in the capitulation.

Though the recovery from his wound was not complete, he repaired to head quarters in the following August, and was joyfully received by the Commander in

Chief. His military reputation was high ; and at the solicitation of the delegates of South Carolina and Georgia, he was designated by Congress to take the command in the southern department. On his arrival at Charleston, in December, 1778, he found that he had to form an army, to provide supplies, and to arrange the various departments, in order to enable him to contend against experienced officers and veteran troops, with any probability of success. For this, his indefatigable perseverance, and unconquerable energy were necessary and excellent qualifications. It is impossible to recount here, all the military operations in this department, in which the skill, prudence and courage of General Lincoln were so conspicuously displayed.

His answer to the British commander, on one occasion, when summoned to surrender, exhibits the modesty and firmness of this estimable officer. "Sixty days (says he) have passed since it has been known that your intentions against this town were hostile, in which time has been afforded to abandon it ; but duty and inclination point to the propriety of supporting it to the last extremity."

But circumstances beyond his controul, rendered it necessary for him to comply with the solicitation of the inhabitants and of others, to accede to capitulation. With all the judicious and vigorous efforts in his power, he was requited with the frowns of fortune ; but he did not in consequence of his ill success, incur the censure of any ; nor was his judgment or merit called in question. He stood high in the confidence of the army, and was esteemed as a zealous patriot and a brave officer. He still enjoyed the undiminished respect of Congress and of the Commander in Chief. Ramsay and Lee speak of his conduct in terms of approbation.

General Lincoln was admitted to his parole, and in November following, he was exchanged for Major General Phillips, a prisoner of the convention at Saratoga. In the campaign of 1781, General Lincoln commanded a division under Washington, and at the siege of Yorktown, he had his full share of the honour of that brilliant event. The articles of capitulation stipulated for the same honour in favour of the surrendering army as had been granted to the garrison at Charleston. General Lincoln was appointed to conduct them to the field where their arms were deposited, and received the customary submission. His services were particularly mentioned in the general order of the Commander in Chief.

In October, 1781, he was chosen by Congress, Secretary of War, retaining his rank in the army. He continued in this office two years, and then resigned. On accepting his resignation, a resolution was adopted in Congress, expressive of their high sense of his perseverance, fortitude, activity and meritorious services in the field, as well as of his diligence, fidelity and capacity in the execution of the office of Secretary of War. After his resignation, General Lincoln retired to his farm in this town; but in 1784, he was chosen one of the commissioners on the part of the State to make a treaty with the Penobscot Indians. In 1786–7, when the insurrection of Shays and Day occurred, General Lincoln was appointed by the governour and council, to command the detachment of militia consisting of four or five thousand men, to oppose the progress of the insurgents, and to compel their submission to the laws. By his address and energy, the insurrection was happily suppressed without much bloodshed.

At the May election, in 1787, General Lincoln was elected lieutenant governour by the Legislature, having had a plurality of votes by the people. He was a member of the convention for ratifying the Constitution of the United States ; and in 1789, he was appointed by President Washington, Collector of the Port of Boston, which office he retained till about two years before his death. In 1789, he was appointed one the commissioners to treat with the Creek Indians, and in 1793, he was one of the commissioners to effect a peace with the Western Indians.

General Lincoln, was one of the first members of the American Academy of Arts and Sciences, and a member of the Massachusetts Historical Society, to each of which he contributed papers for their respective publications. He received from Harvard University, the degree of Master of Arts. He was President of the Society of Cincinnati, from its organization, until his decease.

After his resignation of the office of Collector of Boston, he lived about two years in retirement, and died May 8, 1810.

A writer in the Historical Collections, thus speaks of his character.

"In General Lincoln's character, strength and softness, the estimable and amiable qualities, were happily blended. His mind was quick and active, yet discriminating and sound. He displayed a fund of thought and information derived from select though limited reading, from careful observation of men and things, from habits of thinking and from conversation. A degree of enthusiasm or exaltation of feeling on the objects of his pursuit belonged to his temperament, but it was under the controul of good sense and sober views. He was patient and cool in deliberation, in execution prompt and vigorous. He was conspicuous for plain, strict, inflexible integrity, united however with prudence, candour, and a compassionate disposition. As a military commander, he was judicious, brave, determined, indefatigable. His distinguished merit in this character was never denied, while all have not agreed in opinion on some of his plans in the southern command. Being a soldier of the revolution he had to anticipate the effect of experience, and might commit mistakes. He was surrounded by difficulties; he met extraordinary disappointments in his calculations of supplies and succours. In the principal instances which issued unfortunately, the storming of Savannah and the siege of Charleston, he had but a choice of evils; and which ever way he decided, the course rejected would have seemed to many persons more eligible.

"He was a Christian of the Antisectarian, Catholic, or liberal sect. He was firm in his faith, serious and affectionate in his piety, without superstition, fanaticism or austerity. He was from early manhood a communicant, and for a great part of his life a deacon of the church. He never shunned an avowal of his belief, nor feared to appear what he was, nor permitted the reality of his convictions to remain in doubt. The person and air of General Lincoln betokened his military vocation. He was of a middle height and erect, broad chested and muscular, in his latter years corpulent, with open intelligent features, a venerable and benign aspect. His manners were easy and unaffected, but courteous and polite."*

* The above sketch of the services and character of Gen. Lincoln is principally abridged from histories of the revolution, Mass. His. Collections and Thacher's Military Journal.

SKETCH OF THE LINCOLN FAMILIES.

It is perhaps an object of curiosity and amusement, rather than of instruction, to trace the history of families, and the numerous branches of successive generations to their common origin. There is an interest however, in ascertaining the connecting links which bind us to an ancestry whose virtues are worthy of imitation, and whose principles should be cherished and cultivated by their posterity. These remarks apply to many of the early settlers of Hingham; and it would have been an agreeable employment to have searched among the monuments of our ancestors, and to have gathered more of the fleeting traditions of our aged fathers, relating to the character and services of those who laid the foundations of our civil and social priviliges, as well as of our religious liberties.

The number of the early settlers of Hingham, of the name of Lincoln, and the fact, that all of this name scattered in almost every state in the Union, originated from this village, induces me to give all the information which I have collected relating to them, that others may fill up the outlines and arrange for their own gratification some sketch of their respective ancestors.

The first record which can be found of the arrival in this country of a person by the name of Lincoln, is in the manuscripts of Daniel Cushing. It is as follows:

" 1633. Nicholas Jacob, with his wife and two children and their cousin THOMAS LINCOLN, weaver, came from old Hingham and settled in this Hingham." His grant of a house lot was made by the town in 1636. It was situated on the south side of the " Town street," now South street. He was married twice ; his first wife, Susanna, died in 1641 ; he married Mary Chubbuck, in 1663 ; he died September 2, 1675, leaving no children, and his wife surviving. From a copy of his will in my possession, it appears that he gave the largest portion of his estate to the children of his brother SAMUEL. Of the arrival of SAMUEL LINCOLN in this country, there is the following record in Cushing's MSS. : " 1637. John Tower and Samuel Lincoln came from old Hingham, and both settled at new Hingham ; Samuel Lincoln living some time at Salem." His children were Samuel, Daniel, Mordecai, Mary, Thomas, Martha, Sarah, and Rebecca. Of this family, Samuel (styled the carpenter,) married Deborah Hersey, daughter of William Hersey, (ancestor of Drs. Ezekiel and Abner Hersey.) Their children were Deborah, Samuel, Jedidiah, Mary, Rebecca, Elisha, Lydia, Abigail and Susanna. Of these children, Samuel had sons, Samuel and Jonathan ; Samuel the father of Seth, &c. now living ; and Jonathan father of Ezekiel, Beza, &c. now living. Jedidiah (a glazier,) married Bethiah Whiton, and after her decease Mrs. Barker relict of Capt. Francis Barker. Jedidiah died in the 91st year of his age. The children of Jedidiah and Bethiah, were Jedidiah, Enoch, Mary, William and Levi. Jedidiah, Enoch and William only, lived to manhood. Jedidiah was a respectable citizen, sometimes an assessor, selectman, &c. Enoch married Rachel Fearing, and after her decease, Lydia Ripley relict of Nehemiah Ripley and daughter of Rev. Nehemiah Hobart of Cohasset. Enoch Lincoln, in the early part of his life was a mariner, afterwards a glazier and farmer. He is often mentioned in the sketch of civil history ; he was a zealous and independent whig, a prudent, discreet, shrewd and sensible man. The children of Enoch and Rachel were Bethiah, Enoch; Levi, Rachel, Amos, Sarah, Ezra, Leah, Jedidiah, Abraham and Mary. Bethiah married Jonathan Thaxter ; their children were Jonathan Thaxter of Boston, Hon. Levi Thaxter of Watertown, &c. Levi Lincoln was the Lieut. Governour of Massachusetts, (see p. 126.) Amos, was a member of the celebrated Boston Tea Party, and a captain of Artillery in the Revolutionary War. He is yet living. Leah married the late Hawkes Fearing, Esq. Mr. Fearing was a very useful and influential citizen of Hingham. He was frequently elected to our most important town offices, and was very justly esteemed for his excellent moral character, his unyielding integrity, and his honest independence of mind. He died June 6, 1826. Abraham Lincoln resided at Worcester, filled many public offices, and among them that of Counsellor of this Commonwealth.

William Lincoln, third son of Jedidiah, married Mary Otis, daughter of Ephraim Otis of Scituate. His sons were William, Otis, Henry, H. U. 1786, (see p. 133,) and Solomon, father of the compiler of this sketch—all living.

Mordecai Lincoln, son of the first Samuel, removed within the present limits of Cohasset, and was the ancestor of several families in that town. He had a son Isaac, a grandson Isaac, and a great grandson Uriah, (the late venerable deacon of the church at Cohasset.) Uriah was the father of Isaac Lincoln, M. D., H. U. 1800, physician in Brunswick, Me.

Elisha Lincoln, son of the second Samuel, removed to to Cohasset, and left descendants there.

The name of THOMAS LINCOLN, cooper, appears in our records in 1636. His house lot was the same, which is now owned by his descendant, Martin Lincoln, Esq. at the corner of Lincoln and North streets. Thomas Lincoln had a son Benjamin, and a grandson Benjamin; this Benjamin was the father of Col. Benjamin Lincoln, who died March 1, 1771. Col. Lincoln was the father of General Benjamin Lincoln, of the Revolutionary Army, and of Dr. Bela Lincoln. General Benjamin Lincoln's sons were Benjamin Lincoln, Esq. H. U. 1777, Counsellor at Law, of Boston, (see p. 132,) Theodore Lincoln, H. U. 1785, of Dennysville, Me., and Martin Lincoln, Esq. of Hingham. The last mentioned Benjamin, married a daughter of James Otis. His sons were Dr. Benjamin Lincoln, H. U. 1806, who died at Demarara, a few years since, and James Otis Lincoln, Esq. H. U. 1807, who died in Hingham, August 12, 1818.

The name of THOMAS LINCOLN, Jr., miller, also appears in our records, in 1636. He removed with his family, to Taunton, before the year 1652, as appears by the Plymouth Colony Records. He made his will at Taunton, in 1683, and in it mentions his age, (80 years,) and styles himself grand senior. His children and descendants were numerous, and from him, probably, descended all the persons of the name of Lincoln, in Bristol County. Some of his descendants removed to Connecticut.

The name of THOMAS LINCOLN, the husbandman, appears in our records, in 1638. It is difficult to trace his descendants, although it may not be an impossibility. The singular fact, that four of the same name were among our early settlers, of whom three left numerous descendants, and some of whom probably had children who had nearly arrived to manhood before they came to this country, causes no little embarrassment in perfecting their genealogy. Daniel Lincoln was "one of the young men" a few years after the settlement of the town ; but I have not been able to ascertain of which Thomas Lincoln he was the son. The descendants of Daniel, are numerous and widely scattered through the country. A full account of his descendants is in the possession of Jotham Lincoln, Esq., Town Clerk of Hingham.

The arrival of STEPHEN LINCOLN, to this country, was, according to Cushings MSS. in 1638. His record is as follows : "1638, Steven Lincoln, and his wife, and his son Steven, came from Windham, and settled in New Hingham." The first Stephen had but one son, and three grandsons, viz. : Stephen, (a bachelor,) David and James. The sons of David, were David, Matthew and Isaac Lincoln, H. U. 1722. The sons of the second David, were David, and Nathan. David died February 1, 1814, aged 79. Nathan died, December 19, 1809, aged 71. The sons of David were the following, Dea. David Lincoln, who died August 1825, aged 58, Hawkes, Perez, H. U. 1798, died August 3, 1805, Noah and Ensign. The only son of Nathan was the late Abner Lincoln, Esq.

The sons of Matthew Lincoln, were Stephen, Noah, Job, Matthew, Levi and Isaiah. Stephen's sons were Calvin, Stephen, Elisha : Calvin, the father of Calvin, H. U. 1820.

Matthew had several sons. Those now residing in Hingham, Jedidiah and Hezekiah. The only son of Levi is Dr. Levi Lincoln, H. U. 1789. The sons of Job, Mitchel and Bradford, of Boston, &c.

The sons of Isaac Lincoln, H. U. 1722, were Isaac, James, Nathaniel and Heman. Isaac, the father of Daniel ; James, father of Perez ; Nathaniel, father of the late Capt. Luther Lincoln, (father of Luther B. Lincoln, H. U. 1822,) Bela, Robert, and Martin Lincoln of Ohio ; Heman father of Hon. Heman Lincoln of Boston, and Pyam.*

The longevity of this family has been generally remarkable. For instance, the sons of the first Matthew, died at the following ages :

Isaiah Lincoln	died April 1, 1786,	aged 42 years.†
Noah Lincoln	" Nov. 13, 1810,	" 82 "
Stephen Lincoln	" Nov. 8, 1816,	" 91 "
Job Lincoln	" May 17, 1818,	" 85 "
Levi Lincoln	" May 12, 1819,	" 81 "
Matthew Lincoln	" Dec. 18, 1821,	" 87 "

The ancestors of this aged family lived also to an advanced age.

The preceding sketch of the Lincoln families probably embraces all the heads of familes among the early settlers. There may be omissions in the names of their descendants ; it is not pretended to be perfectly full, but is probably accurate as far as it extends.

* For this account of the descendants of Stephen Lincoln, I am indebted to Jedidiah Lincoln, Esq. one of his descendants.

† Isaiah Lincoln was killed by an accident, and should not be considered in the statement.

SKETCH OF THE WILDER FAMILIES.

In a "Note on the Wilders," in the History of Lancaster, written by Joseph Willard, Esq., I find the following account of the Lancaster tradition respecting this family.

"The tradition of the family is that Thomas Wilder, the first of the name in this country, came from Lancaster in England; that he settled in Hingham, and had four sons, that one son remained in Hingham, from whom are descended all of the name of Wilder in that town and vicinity. I find that Thomas Wilder was made freeman, 2d June, 1641, and that he was of Charlestown in 1642. One named Edward, took the freeman's oath, 29th May, 1644, and was afterwards of Hingham (2. Mass. Hist. Col. 4. 221), but whether, or how related to Thomas I do not know."

The first part of this account is entirely irreconcileable with any tradition among the Wilder families in this place. The traditionary account which I have collected here, is as follows: "A widow woman, by the name of Wilder, came out of England, with two boys, her only children; having before their departure disposed of their entailed estate; and she never would disclose to her son Edward, who settled with her in Hingham, nor to any other person that we know of, the name of the place in

England from which they came. Our ancestors have not left us any uniform tradition respecting the other boy ; some of them supposing that he must have been the Wilder from whom descended the families of that name in Lancaster and its vicinity : the conjecture of others is, that he died on his passage to this country, or soon after his arrival, &c."

This account of the tradition of the family here, was given me by Messrs. Joseph Wilder and Joshua Wilder, to the former of whom I am indebted for other traditionary information.

On an examination of our town records, I find that Widow ———— Wilder received a grant of a house lot, in 1638. Prior to 1664, Edward Wilder received a grant of land near that which his mother had received from the town ; and by a subsequent conveyance of the premises, in which a reference is made to the grant to his mother, it appears that her name was Martha. She died April 20, 1652. Her son, Edward Wilder, was the ancestor of all the Wilders in this place. He married Elizabeth Ames, of Marshfield, before 1654, and had four sons and four daughters. He died, October 18, 1690 ; his wife died, June 9, 1692. A perfect list of his male descendants who lived to manhood, to the fifth generation, has been given me by the gentlemen before mentioned, which I subjoin as a matter of mere curiosity. Those with an asterisk affixed, died without issue.—Families are separated by a dash, and arranged according to seniority.

Second generation.—Edward's sons—John, Ephraim,* Isaac and Jabez.

Third generation—Ephraim, Isaac,—Thomas,—Jabez,* Edward and Theophilus.

Fourth generation—Ephraim, John, David, Abel,* Seth,—Isaac, Daniel,—Nathaniel, Thomas, Samuel,

Isaac,—Edward, Joseph, Isaiah, Benjamin,—Jabez, Theophilus, Zenas.

Fifth generation—Ephraim,* Peter,*—John, Zechariah, Abel, Lot, Elias, Stephen,—David, Shubael,—Seth, Abel, —Isaac, Laban, Calvin, Cushing, John,—Daniel, Abiel, Joseph,——Nathaniel,——Thomas, Nathaniel,——James,* Samuel,—Bela, Eleazer, Isaac, Jairus,—Edward, Lewis, Joshua, Martin, Benjamin,—Joseph,—Isaiah,—Josiah,* John, Lewis, Peter, Benjamin, James, Harrison,— Crocker, Warren, Jabez,—Theophilus, Ebenezer, Bela, Theodore,—Zenas, Theophilus, Pyam, Ephraim.

By comparing these names with those of the Lancaster Wilders, it appears to me conclusive, that they had a common ancestor ; and I think there can be little doubt that the brother of our first Edward, was Thomas Wilder of Lancaster.

SKETCH OF THE HOBART FAMILIES.

Edmund Hobart, who arrived at Charlestown in 1633, was the ancestor of all the Hobarts in this place and vicinity. He settled in this place in 1635, and died March 8, 1645–6. The children of Edmund, were Edmund, Thomas, Peter and Joshua, and two daughters. Edmund Hobart, Jr. died in 1686, aged 82 ; Samuel, Daniel and John were his children. Thomas Hobart had sons, Caleb, Joshua and Thomas. Peter Hobart, the first minister of Hingham, a native of Hingham, England, in 1604, was educated at the University at Cambridge, England ; after he left the University, he taught a grammar school, and preached in Hingham, England, for nine years, when he came to this country.

Rev. Peter Hobart was the father of "a celebrated progeny of divines," all of whom have been noticed in previous parts of this work. The late Judge John Sloss Hobart of New York, was a great grandson of Rev. Peter Hobart ; and I think that the present distinguished Bishop of New York, John H. Hobart, D. D. is connected with this branch of the Hobart family. Japheth Hobart, who died January 17, 1822, aged 94, was a great grandson of Rev. Peter Hobart. The children of Capt. Joshua Hobart, who died July 28, 1682, were Joshua, Enoch, (and Solomon, probably,) and two daughters, one of whom married Edward Cowell, and the other Joshua Lincoln.

Isaac Hobart, son of Aaron, a descendant of the first Edmund, removed to Abington in 1724; he died in 1775. His sons were Thomas Hobart, Col. Aaron Hobart and John Hobart. Thomas Hobart, Esq. and Isaac Hobart of Hanson, are sons of this Thomas. Seth, Aaron, Noah, Isaac and Jacob, were sons of Col. Aaron Hobart. Seth, father of Nathaniel, H. U. 1784; Aaron, father of Hon. Aaron Hobart, B. U. 1805, late member of Congress; Noah, father of Albert, Nathaniel, James, and Aaron Hobart, of Charleston, S. C.; Isaac Hobart resides at Eastport; Benjamin Hobart, B. U. 1804, is a son of Col. Aaron Hobart. A full sketch of this numerous and respectable family would fill a volume, and I must leave it imperfect and unfinished. The first settlers of this name are given; and from those, nothing is required but time and patience, to trace a perfect genealogy.

LONGEVITY.

Our town records do not furnish a correct list of the deaths in this place until within a few years; the record of Rev. Peter Hobart does not give the ages of persons whose deaths are recorded; and the perfect record of Dr. Gay embraces only those who died in his parish; hence we have no exact data from which to estimate the proportion of deaths to the whole population, for any given time previous to the present century. The average number of deaths within a few years past is about fifty, being one in sixty of the inhabitants. The town has been afflicted with no epidemics for a long series of years. The number of deaths in the alms house from 1786 to 1826, (inclusive) was 118. The ages of 115 recorded, average upwards of 62 years, to each person. Of those, 10 were 90 years of age and upwards, and 27 of them 80 and upwards.

The oldest person that ever lived in Hingham, was Daniel Stodder, who died in 1737, in the 104th year of his age. Several have died at the age of 100 years, as, Theophilus Cushing in 1678-9; Hannah Johnson, in 1728, &c. Hingham is probably one of the most healthy towns in the commonwealth.

APPENDIX.

INDIAN DEED.

(See page 81.)

WHEREAS divers Englishmen did formerly come (into the Massachusets now called by the Englishmen New England) to inhabit in the dayes of Chickatabut our father who was the Cheife Sachem of the sayd Massachusets on the Southward side of Charles River, and by the free Consent of our sayd father did set downe upon his land and in the yeare of our Lord God one thousand six hundred thirty and four divers Englishmen did set downe and inhabit upon part of the land that was formerly our sayd fathers land, which land the Englishmen call by the name of Hingham, which sayd Englishmen they and their heires and assosiats have ever since had quiet and peaceable possession of their Towneshippe of Hingham by our likeing and Consent which we desire they may still quietly possess and injoy and because ther have not yet bin any legall conveyance in writing passed from us to them conserning their land which may in future time occasion difference between them and us all which to prevent——Know all men by these presents that we Wompatuck called by the English Josiah now Cheife Sachem of the Massachusets aforesayd and sonne and heire to the aforesayd Chickatabut: and Squmuck all called by the English Daniel sonne of the aforesayd Chickatabut and Ahahden—Indians: for a valueable consideration to us in hand payd by Captaine Joshua Hubberd and Ensigne John Thaxter, of Hingham aforesayd wherewith wee doe acknowledge our selves fully satisfyed contented and payd and thereof and of every part and percell thereof doe exonerate acquitt and discharge the sayd Joshua Hubberd and John Thaxter their heires executors and Administrators and every of them forever by these presents : have given granted bargained sold enfeoffed and confirmed and by these presents doe give grant bargaine sell Enfeoffe and confirme unto the sayd Joshua Hubberd and John Thaxter on the behalfe and to the use of the inhabitants of the Towne of Hingham aforesayd that is to say all such as are the present owners and proprietors of the present house lotts as they have bin from time to time granted and layd out by the Towne : All That Tract of land which is the Towneshippe of Hingham aforesayd as it is now bounded with the sea northward and with the River called by the Englishmen weymoth River westward which River flow from the sea : and the line that devide betwene the sayd Hingham and Weymoth as it is now layd out and marked untill it come to the line that devide betwene the colony of the Massachusets and the colony of New Plimoth and from thence to the midle of accord pond and from the midle of accord pond to bound Brooke to the flowing of the salt water and so along by the same River that devide betwene Scittiate and the said Hingham untill it come to the sea northward : And also threescore acres of salt marsh on the other side of the River that is to say on Scittiate side according as it was agreed upon by the commissioners of the Massachusets colony and the commissioners of Plimoth colony Together with all the Harbours Rivers Creekes Coves Islands fresh water brookes and ponds and all marshes unto the sayd Towneshippe of Hingham belonging or any wayes app'taineing with all and singular thapp'tenences unto the p'misses or any part of them belonging or any wayes app'taineing : And all our right title and interest of and into the sayd p'misses with their app'tenences and every part and p'cell thereof to have and to hold All the aforesayd Tract of land which is the Towneshippe of Hingham aforesayd and is bounded as aforesayd with all the Harbours Rivers Creekes Coves Islands fresh water brookes and ponds and all marshes ther unto belonging with the threescore acres of salt marsh on the other side of the River (viz) on Scittiate side with all and singular thapp'tenences to the sayd p'misses or any of them belonging unto the sayd Joshua Hubberd and John Thaxter on the behalfe and to the use of the sayd inhabitants who are the present owners and proprietors of the present house lotts in hingham their heires and assignes from the before named time in the yeare of our Lord God one thousand six hundred thirty and four for ever And unto the only proper use and behoofe of the [the] sayd Joshua hubberd and John Thaxter and the inhabitants of the Towne of hingham who are the present owners and proprietors of the present house lotts in the Towne of Hingham their heires and assignes for ever. And the said Wompatuck Squmuck and Ahahden doe hereby covenant promise and grant to and with the sayd Joshua hubberd and John Thaxter on the behalfe of the inhabitants of hingham as aforesayd that they the sayd Wompatuck Squmuck and Ahahdun—are the true and proper owners of the sayd bargained p'misses with their app'tenances at the time of the bargaine and sale thereof and that the sayd bargained p'misses are free and cleare and freely and clearely exonerated acquitted and discharged of and from all and all maner of former bargaines sales guifts grants titles mortgages suits attachments actions Judgements extents executions dowers title of dowers and all other incumberances whatsoever from the begining of the world untill the time of the bargaine and sale thereof and that the sayd Joshua hubberd and John Thaxter with the rest of the sayd inhabitants who are the present owners and proprietors of the present house lotts in hingham they their heires and Assignes the p'misses and every part and parcell thereof shall quietly have hold use occupy possese and injoy without the let suit trouble deniall or molestation of them the sayd Wompatuck : Squmuck and Ahahdun their heires and assignes : and Lastly the sayd Wompatuck : Squmuck and Ahahdun for themselves their heires executors administrators and assignes doe hereby covenant promise and grant the p'misses above demised with all the libertys previledges and app'tenences thereto or in any wise belonging or appertaineing unto the sayd Joshua Hubberd John Thaxter and the rest of the sayd inhabitants of Hingham who are the present owners and proprietors of the present house lotts their heires and assignes to warrant acquitt and defend forever against all and all maner of right title and Interrest claime or demand of all and every person or persons whatsoever And that it shall and may be lawfull to and for the sayd Joshua Hubberd and John Thaxter their heires and assignes to record and enroll or cause to be recorded and enrolled the title and tenour of these p'sents according to

APPENDIX.

the usuall order and maner of recording and enrolling deeds and evedences in such case made and p'vided in witnes whereof we the aforesayd Wompatuck called by the English Josiah sachem : and Squmuck called by the English Daniell and Ahahdun Indians: have heere unto set our hands and scales the fourth day of July in the yeare of our Lord God one thousand six hundred sixty and five and in the seaventeenth yeare of the raigne of our soveraigne Lord Charles the second by the grace of God of Great Brittanie France and Ireland King defender of the faith &c 1665 - - -
Signed scalled and delivered
In the the presence of us:

Job Noeshteans Indian	the marke ⚹O of (L.S.) Wompatuck called by the English Josiah cheif sachem
the marke of W william Manananianut Indian	
the marke of 8 Robert Mamuntahgin Indian	the marke ⚹ of Squmuck (L.S.) called by the English Daniell sonne of Chickatabut
John Hues	
Mattias Q Briggs	the marke ⚏ of Ahahden (L.S.)
the marke of ⌐ Job Judkins	

Josiah Wompatuck Squmuck Ahahden Indians apeared p'sonally the 19th of may 1668 and acknowledged this instrum't of writing to be theyr act and deed freely and voluntary without compulsion, acknowledged before JNO. LEVERETT, Ast.

☞The above copy of the Indian Deed of the Township of Hingham, is printed literally and verbally, from the original.

REPRESENTATIVES.

Supposing that a correct list of representatives of this town, in the General Court, &c. from 1636 to the present time might not be uninteresting, I have prepared the following list. James Savage, Esq. politely furnished that portion of it which extends from May 1636 to 1666. In a few cases the delegates were not inhabitants of Hingham, as Blackleach, in 1636, Houchin, in 1651, &c., Savage, in 1663.

At the sixth Court,
25 May, 1636, Mr. Blackleach, Joseph Andrews, Nicholas Baker.
8 Sept. " Joseph Andrews.
7 Dec. " none
18 April 37, Joseph Andrews, Anthony Eames.
17 May, " Joseph Andrews, Anthony Eames.
26 Sept. " Joseph Andrews, Anthony Eames.
2 Nov. " Samuel Warde.
12 March, " Samuel Warde, Anthony Eames.
2 May, 38, Joseph Andrews, Nicholas Baker.
6 Sept. " Mr. Joseph Hull, Anthony Eames.
13 March, " Mr. Joseph Hull, Anthony Eames.
22 May, 39, Mr. Joseph Peck, Edmund Hobart.
4 Sept. " Mr. Joseph Peck, Edmund Hobart.
13 May, 40, Mr. Joseph Peck, Mr. James Bates.
7 Oct. " Mr. Joseph Peck, Edmund Hobart.
2 June, 41, Mr. Joseph Peck, Henry Smyth.
8 Oct. " Mr. Joseph Peck, Stephen Paine.

The deputies at the General Court from Oct. 1641 to Sept. 1642 do not appear in the Records, as there is a slight failure in the beginning of Vol. II.

8 Sept. 1642, Mr. Joseph Peck, Edmund Hobart.
10 May. 43, Bozoan Allen, Joshua Hobart.
7 March, " Anthony Eames, Joshua Hobart.
29 May, 44, Bozoan Allen, John Porter.
14 " 45, Bozoan Allen, Joshua Hobart.
6 " 46, Bozoan Allen, Joshua Hobart.
26 " 47, Bozoan Allen, Joshua Hobart.
10 " 48, Nicholas Jacob, Thomas Underwood.
2 " 49, Nicholas Jacob, John Beale.
22 " 50, Bozoan Allen, Joshua Hobart.
7 " 51, Bozoan Allen, Jeremiah Houchin.*
27 " 52, Bozoan Allen, Jeremiah Houchin.
18 " 53, Joshua Hobart, Jeremiah Houchin.

* Jeremiah Houchin, was a citizen of Boston, and sometimes a selectman of the town:—" Jeremy Houchin, who was a tanner by trade, was located at the corner of Hanover and Court streets (Concert Hall) and had his tan-pits and tan-yards there."—*Snow's History of Boston.*

APPENDIX.

		1721,	Nathaniel Hobart.
3	Aug.	"	Thomas Loring.
11	May,	22,	Thomas Loring.
26	April,	23,	Thomas Loring.
1	May,	24,	Thomas Loring.
3	"	25,	Thomas Loring.
9	"	26,	John Jacob, re-elected for the seven years following.
13	"	34,	James Hearsey.
19	"	35,	James Hearsey.
17	"	36,	James Hearsey.
9	"	37,	Jacob Cushing.*
17	"	38,	Jacob Cushing.
14	"	39,	Jacob Cushing.
14	"	40,	Jacob Cushing.
13	"	41,	John Jacob.
17	"	42,	Thomas Gill.
9	"	43,	Thomas Gill.
14	"	44,	Thomas Gill.
20	Aug.	"	Jacob Cushing, " in room of Thomas Gill, Esq. who is gone into his Majesty's service."—*Town Records*.
13	May,	1745,	Jacob Cushing.
12	"	46,	Benjamin Lincoln.
18	"	47,	Benjamin Lincoln.
12	"	48,	Benjamin Lincoln.
10	"	49,	Jacob Cushing, re-elected for the eight following years.
25	"	58,	Joshua Hearsey, re-elected for the *thirteen* following years.
18	"	72,	John Thaxter.
19	"	73,	Benjamin Lincoln.
18	"	74,	Benjamin Lincoln.
21	Sept.	"	Benjamin Lincoln, to the Court to be held at Salem.
21	Sept.	74,	Benjamin Lincoln, chosen to represent the town in the Provincial Congress to be held at Concord.

* Jacob Cushing, Esq. a respectable magistrate of this town, died in 1777, aged 82.

APPENDIX. 167

26 Dec. 1774, Benjamin Lincoln, chosen to represent the town in the Provincial Congress to be held at Cambridge.
24 May, 75, Benjamin Lincoln, chosen to represent the town in the Congress at Watertown.
10 July, 75, Benjamin Lincoln, chosen to represent the town in the General Court to be held at Watertown agreeably to a resolve of the Provincial Congress.
16 Aug. 75, Enoch Lincoln, chosen to represent the town in the General Court then sitting at Watertown.
23 May, 76, Enoch Lincoln, Theophilus Cushing, and John Fearing, chosen representatives to the next General Court.
20 May, 77, Enoch Lincoln, chosen representative to the General Court.
18 May, 78, Enoch Lincoln, Joseph Thaxter.
17 " 79, Joseph Thaxter, Jr. Mr. Thaxter, resigned his seat, and the vacancy was not filled.
22 May, 80, Charles Cushing.*

UNDER THE CONSTITUTION.

9 Oct. 1780, Charles Cushing.
14 May, 81, Charles Cushing.
13 " 82, Theophilus Cushing.†
12 " 83, Theophilus Cushing.
10 " 84, Charles Cushing.
9 " 85, Theophilus Cushing.
8 " 86, Theophilus Cushing.
14 " 87, Theophilus Cushing.
5 " 88, Benjamin Lincoln, Theophilus Cushing.
4 " 89, Benjamin Lincoln.
3 " 90, Charles Cushing.
2 " 91, Charles Cushing.

* Col. Charles Cushing was one of the most influential and respectable of the whigs of the Revolution, in this town. He was a gentleman of excellent natural abilities, zealous and persevering in whatever engaged. He removed from this town to Lunenburg, in Worcester County, in 1797, where he died, November 25, 1809, aged 65.
† Gen. Theophilus Cushing, died March 11, 1820.

APPENDIX.

7 May,   1792, Charles Cushing.
6 "   93, Charles Cushing.
5 "   94, Theophilus Cushing.
6 "   95, Samuel Norton.
2 "   96, Samuel Norton.
1 "   97, Samuel Norton.
7 "   98, Jacob Leavitt.
6 "   99, Jotham Gay.*
5 "   1800, Jotham Gay.
4 "   01, Nathan Rice,† re-elected for the three following years.
6 "   05, Nathan Rice, Levi Lincoln.
5 "   06, Hawkes Fearing.
4 "   07, Hawkes Fearing.
2 "   08, Hawkes Fearing, Jonathan Cushing.
1 "   09, Hawkes Fearing, Jonathan Cushing, and Thomas Fearing.‡ The same gentlemen were re-elected in 1810 and 11.
4 "   12, Thomas Fearing, Jonathan Cushing, Jotham Lincoln, Jr.
3 "   13, The same as last year.
2 "   14, Thomas Fearing.
1 "   15, Thomas Fearing.
6 "   16, Thomas Fearing, Jedidiah Lincoln, Charles W. Cushing.
5 "   17, Thomas Fearing.
4 "   18, Jedidiah Lincoln.
3 "   19, Jedidiah Lincoln.
1 "   20, James Stephenson, Solomon Jones.
7 "   21, James Stephenson, Solomon Jones, Joseph Richardson.§
6 "   22   Joseph Richardson.

* Col. Jotham Gay, son of Ebenezer Gay, D. D. He died October 16, 1802.
† Col. Nathan Rice, of the Army of the Revolution. H. U. 1773.
‡ Dea. Thomas Fearing died March 16, 1820, aged 70.
§ Mr. Richardson was elected a member of the Senate of this Commonwealth in 1823, and re-elected in 1824. He was again elected in 1826; and he now represents Plymouth District in the twentieth Congress.

APPENDIX. 169

5 "   23, Jedidiah Lincoln, John Leavitt, Isaiah Wilder.
3 "   24, Isaiah Wilder, Benjamin Thomas.
2 "   25, Benjamin Thomas. Mr. Thomas was re-elected in 1826 and 1827.

Delegates to the Convention, for revising the Constitution in 1820-1, Joseph Richardson, Jotham Lincoln, Thomas Fearing.*

* Thomas Fearing, Esq. a magistrate, and a very estimable citizen, died March 29, 1827, aged 48.

TOWN CLERKS.

For the subjoined list of Town Clerks of Hingham, I am indebted to Jotham Lincoln, Esq.
Joseph Andrews, elected in 1637.
Matthew Hawke, died December 11, 1684.
Daniel Cushing, elected Dec. 21, 1669, died Dec. 3, 1700.
James Hawke, elected Dec. 26, 1700, died Nov. 27, 1715.
Stephen Lincoln, elected July 27, 1716, died Dec. 27, 1717.
John Norton, elected Dec. 31, 1717, died August 5, 1721.
Benjamin Lincoln, elected Aug. 24, 1721, died July 10, 1727.
Benjamin Lincoln, elected July 24, 1727.
Benjamin Lincoln, Jr. elected March 7, 1757.
Benjamin Cushing, elected March 3, 1778, died Aug. 8, 1812.
Solomon Jones, elected March 10, 1806.
Jotham Lincoln, elected March 10, 1823.

☞ Samuel Norton officiated as Clerk *pro tempore*, from July 1776, to March, 1778.

VOTES FOR GOVERNOUR,

Given in Hingham, since the adoption of the Constitution. The votes for the two leading candidates only are given:

Year	Candidate	Votes	Candidate	Votes
1780,	John Hancock	44,	James Bowdoin	12
81,	John Hancock	36,		
82,	John Hancock	41,	James Bowdoin	9
83,	Benjamin Lincoln	31,	John Hancock	7
84,	James Bowdoin	26,	John Hancock	23
85,	Benjamin Lincoln	29,	James Bowdoin	27
86,	James Bowdoin	51,		
87,	James Bowdoin	56,	John Hancock	26
88,	John Hancock	72,	James Bowdoin	1
89,	James Bowdoin	60,	Benjamin Lincoln	22
90,	James Bowdoin	39,	John Hancock	7
91,	John Hancock	21,	Thomas Russell	13
92,	Francis Dana	31,	John Hancock	13
93,	Elbridge Gerry	31,	John Hancock	10
94,	William Cushing	95,	Samuel Adams	4
95,	Samuel Adams	36,	William Cushing	35
96,	Increase Sumner	71,	Samuel Adams	16
97,	Increase Sumner	72,	James Sullivan	3
98,	Increase Sumner	95,	James Sullivan	2
99,	Increase Sumner	113,	William Heath	31
1800,	Caleb Strong	76,	Elbridge Gerry	60
01,	Eldridge Gerry	89,	Caleb Strong	74
02,	Elbridge Gerry	97,	Caleb Strong	86
03,	Caleb Strong	102,	Elbridge Gerry	32
04,	Caleb Strong	99,	James Sullivan	60
05,	Caleb Strong	141,	James Sullivan	76
06,	James Sullivan	139,	Caleb Strong	129
07,	James Sullivan	199,	Caleb Strong	135
08,	James Sullivan	232,	Christopher Gore	140
09,	Levi Lincoln	253,	Christopher Gore	140
10,	Elbridge Gerry	249,	Christopher Gore	138
11,	Elbridge Gerry	245,	Christopher Gore	138
12,	Elbridge Gerry	245,	Caleb Strong	171

13,	Joseph B. Varnum	255,		Caleb Strong	195
14,	Samuel Dexter	237,		Caleb Strong	191
15,	Samuel Dexter	204,		Caleb Strong	171
16,	Samuel Dexter	237,		John Brooks	163
17,	Henry Dearborn	221,		John Brooks	153
18,	B.W. Crowninshield	193,		John Brooks	144
19,	B.W. Crowninshield	223,		John Brooks	158
20,	William Eustis	208,		John Brooks	141
21,	William Eustis	202,		John Brooks	146
22,	William Eustis	214,		John Brooks	135
23,	William Eustis	254,		Harrison G. Otis	153
24,	William Eustis	290,		Samuel Lathrop	164
25,	Levi Lincoln	245,		Marcus Morton	16
26,	Levi Lincoln	245,		Samuel Hubbard	39
27,	Levi Lincoln	212,		Harrison G. Otis	19

FREDERICK HENRY IBBEKIN.

The subjoined copy of a letter from Dr. Waterhouse to the late Dr. Barker, of this town, relates to FREDERICK HENRY IBBEKIN, who resided several years since in this town, and who amused himself in constructing machines to enable him to fly. Not succeeding in his experiments, and his funds being exhausted, he shot himself February 13, 1796. The letter may afford some interest to those who knew this unfortunate gentleman:

"*Cambridge, Mass. Feb. 23, 1796.*

"DEAR SIR—Day before yesterday I received your letter. I waited for more information respecting the unfortunate stranger, who is the subject of it, or you would have had an answer by the person who brought it.

"I knew not the name of the gentleman you enquire after, until I heard he had shot himself at Hingham, and that he had left a letter and some papers directed to me. All that I know of him I shall relate.

"About two months since he came to my house alone, and introduced himself with saying that he was a foreigner, and wished an acquaintance with some scientific man: that he understood I had travelled much in foreign countries, and for such and such reasons, which he mentioned, he chose to introduce himself to me in order to converse on a subject which had long been the object of his contemplation. The subject was *pneumatics* and *mechanics*. On these branches of science he talked sensibly and learnedly. Sometimes he spoke in French, sometimes Dutch, and frequently expressed himself in Latin. But what gave the whole a light and whimsical air, was its ultimate application; which was neither more nor less than FLYING *like a bird!* I endeavoured to convince him, that the structure or anatomy of a bird was very different, even in their bones, from man, and from all animals that do not fly; and that amongst other peculiarities, I would remind him that there was no instance in the vast tribe of animated nature, where there was such an *extent of surface*, and such *strength*, united with such *levity*, as are found in the body of a bird; and I expatiated on the anatomy of a quill and of a feather, and of their faculty of filling each tube with air; and that I could not believe that any wings could be contrived, whether like that of a bird's, or like a *bat's*, (which was his favourite notion,) that could raise the human body from the ground, by merely taking hold of the air. He then said he would remove my doubts by actual experiment, and took his leave, with a promise of calling again in three days. He came accordingly, and explained himself farther on his favorite scheme. I listened to him with attention because he seemed to think, in general, like a man of sense, and speak like a gentleman. I could however discern that his *Cartesian* philosophy had not been sufficiently corrected by later demonstrations.

From his good figure, dress, and address, polite and easy manners, I concluded that he was some unfortunate emigrant from the Continent of Europe, probably an officer in the service of the monarchy, who, destitute of money and friends, chose to apply some of the principles he had learnt at college, to the purpose of procuring subsistence by a novel exhibition. On this account I never asked his name or nation.

You ask me, if I suppose he was insane any time before he committed that shocking deed? The writings and drawings which he left directed to me, are so far from evincing a deranged mind, that they indicate a cool and vigorous intellect, being executed not merely with taste, but mathematical exactness. Nevertheless had I been on the Jury, I should have given my verdict "*insanity;*" for he shot himself in a *paroxysm of despair,* which implies a *suspension of reason.*

"I have been told that this unfortunate man quitted his home (*Germany,*) in consequence of his father insisting that he should pursue the profession of divinity. I have never heard any thing against his character; but have seen some evidences of his humanity in giving freedom to his slave, after binding him to a trade by which he could get his living. On the whole I take him to have been one of those unfortunate young men, who having seen but the superficies of life, believed every thing to be what it appears; and whose rapid imagination conceived certain *ends,* without possessing fortune, or patience to pursue the *means.*

"He expresses himself to the following effect in the melancholy letter which he left to me: '*All my plans having failed, my money gone, I resolved to put an end to my life; but thought it my duty to leave to you the description of my machines. My death will make no one unhappy, therefore I go with satisfaction out of this world. Good sir! live well and contented;—when you receive this, I shall be in another world, where I expect to enjoy more happiness than I have experienced in this!*'

"With the horror such a deed naturally inspires, we cannot but mix a portion of commiseration; especially when we recollect that the gifts of a vivid imagination bring the heaviest task on the vigilance of reason; and that such endowments require a degree of discipline, which seldom attends the higher gifts of the mind; clearly proving to us, that *nature,* without the commanding voice of *religion,* has left the noblest of her works imperfect.

"With esteem, &c.

BENJAMIN WATERHOUSE."

To Dr. Barker, Hingham.

SOME ACCOUNT OF THE GILMANS, LEAVITTS, OTISES, &C. &C.

The following is an extract of a letter which I have recently received from JOHN FARMER, Esq. of Concord, New-Hampshire. The information which it contains respecting some of the descendants of the first settlers of Hingham, is too interesting to be withheld from publication.

" Concord, N. H. 15 Dec. 1827.

" Our state is under considerable obligations for the accession we received from the early settlers of Hingham. You are probably aware that the Folsoms, Gilmans and Leavitts, so extensively scattered over New Hampshire, are descended from those of the same name among the first inhabitants of Hingham. Of the first name, there were John, Peter, Ephraim and Samuel in Exeter in 1683, and from these, it is probable, General NATHANIEL FOLSOM, a meritorious officer in our revolutionary war, a state counsellor in 1776, and a delegate to the old Congress, the late Hon. SIMEON FOLSOM, a senator in our legislature for the second district, and Hon. JOHN FOLSOM, late a judge of the court of sessions, are descendants.

" Edward Gilman's descendants are figuratively as numerous as the sands on the sea shore. There is hardly a state in the union in which they may not be found. In 1683, I find there were three families of the name at Exeter, Edward Gilman, John, sen. and John, jr., and these in 1739, had multiplied to more than thirty families of the patronymick name, living in Exeter, besides those who had emigrated to other towns.

" Twenty-four of the grantees of Gilmanton in this state, a town granted in 1727, were of the name of Gilman. The family have been in civil office from the time our colony became a royal province, in 1680, to the present time. JOHN GILMAN was one of the first counsellors named in President Cutts's commission, and died in 1708. Col. PETER GILMAN was one of the royal counsellors in 1772 ; Hon. NICHOLAS GILMAN, a counsellor in 1777 and 1778, Hon. JOSEPH GILMAN, in 1787 ; while the present venerable JOHN TAYLOR GILMAN was fourteen years, eleven in succession, our highly respected Chief Magistrate, his brother NICHOLAS GILMAN, a member of the House of Representatives in Congress eight years, and in the national Senate nine years, and another brother the present NATHANIEL GILMAN a state senator and state treasurer many years. Our ecclesiastical annals have also the Rev. NATHANIEL GILMAN, H. C. 1724, and Rev. TRISTRAM GILMAN, H. C. 1757, both respected clergymen and useful men.

"Samuel and Moses Leavitt, sons of your ancient Dea. John Leavitt, settled in Exeter, and were living there in 1683, and their descendants are numerous, and have enjoyed civil and military office. The late Gen. MOSES LEAVITT, for seven years a senator in the General Court, the present THOMAS LEAVITT, one of the Justices of the Peace throughout the state, and DUDLEY LEAVITT, the astronomer and mathematician of our region, are among their descendants.

"To your list of Graduates, which will form an interesting part of your History, I cannot add, excepting that Rev. Jeremiah Hobart was settled in Hempstead, according to Mr. Wood, in 1682, and removed to Haddam about 1696; and Rev. Jeremiah Cushing, of Scituate, died 22 March, 1706.

"Among the settlers of Hingham under 1635, I notice the name of William Walton. Was not this the Rev. William Walton, mentioned by Johnson, and erroneously called William *Waltham*, by Mather, who was for about twenty years the minister of Marblehead, although not inducted into the pastoral office in that place? I believe some of his descendants are in this state.

"The Otises were here as early as 1663, and the name is common in the county of Strafford. Richard Otis is, I suppose, the common ancestor of all of the name in New Hampshire; and he might have been the son of your John Otis. The name was written on our early records Oates. The names of Hilliard and Hull were here about the same time with that of Otis, and the late Rev. Timothy Hilliard, of Cambridge, was a native of your state, and perhaps a descendant of Emanuel (or Anthony) Hilliard, who was lost, with seven other persons, in a boat going out of Hampton, 20th October, 1657. Ben or Reuben Hull (written both ways) was the ancestor of the Hulls, a name not now common in this region."

ERRATA.

Page 14, line 15, for 1780 read 1788.
" 16, " 14, for June 19, read June 17.

INDEX.

A.

Academy, Derby, 15—19.
Accord Pond, 7.
Agricultural Society, 11.
Allen, Bozoan, 46, 56--70.
Andrews, Joseph 41, 42.
Andrews, Rev. Jedidiah, 116.
Andrews, Rev. John, 138,
Andrews, Lt. Joseph, 111,
Assessors, First record of, 51,
Austin, Jonas, 42.

B.

Baker, Nicholas, 42,
Baptisms, in Gay's ministry, 30 ; in Ware's ministry, 30.
Baptists, 40,
Bare Cove, 22, 40 ; assessment on, 41.
Barker, Capt. Joshua, 91.
Barker, Dr. Joshua, 125—126.
Bates, Joseph deacon, 35.
Beal, John, 44.
Beal, Lazarus deacon, 35.
Beal, Israel, 105, 106, 107.
Bozworth, Jonathan, 45.
Bronson, George, 136.
Brooks, Rev. Charles, 39, 137.

Brown, Rev. John, 36.
Burr, Simon, 48.
Burr, Thomas, 90.

C.

Cade, James, 42.
Canada expedition, troops furnished for, 89.
Chaffe, Thomas, 45.
Child, Dr. Robert, 73—76.
Child, Maj. John, 74.
Chubbuck, Jeremiah, 119.
Church, first, 21—32; at Cohasset 32—36; second, 36—37; third, 39.
Clapp, Thomas, 45.
Cockerum, William, 43.
Cohasset, church at, 32—36; meeting house, 32, 33—34; lands divided, 82; settlement of 82—83.
Colman, Rev. Henry, 39.
Constitution of Massachusetts, report on, &c. 108—109.
Cooper, Thomas, 46.
Cushing, Matthew his decendants, 46.
Cushing, Daniel, 40, 69, 70, 138—139.
Cushing, Rev. Jeremiah, 116, 175.
Cushing, Rev. Job, 116.
Cushing, Adam, 116—117.
Cushing, Matthew, 122.
Cushing, Theophilus, 105, 106, 107.
Cushing, Isaiah, 134.
Cushing, Col. Charles 167.

D.

Day, James, 19.
Deaths in Gay's ministry, 30; in Ware's ministry, 30.
Derby, Mrs. Sarah, 15—19.
Dimock, Thomas, 45.

E.

Eames Anthony, 44, 56—71.
Episcopalians, 40.
Exempts, companies of in the late war, 113.

F.

Fearing, John, 43.
Fearing, John another, 105, 106, 107.
Fearing, Thomas, 169.
Fisk, Mr. Samuel, 25.
Fiske, Dr. R. T. P. 137.

Forts, 84.
Foulshame or Folsom, John, 69, 174.
Fowle, Thomas, 74.
Fowle, Rev. John, 35.
French War, 90—91.
French, Samuel, 123.

G.

Garrison Houses, 84.
Gates, Stephen, 49.
Gay, Rev. Ebenezer, 26—30.
Gay, Samuel, 123.
Gay, Hon. Ebenezer, 137.
Gill, Thomas, 90.
Gill, Thomas another, 119.
Gilman, Edward, 45 ; his descendants, 174-175.
Glad Tidings Plain, why so named, 83.
Gold, Edmund, 69, 70.
Gordon, William A. 136,
Gordon, Charles, 136.
Gordon, Dr. William, 137.
Graduates at different Universities, 113—136.
Grants of land, 49.

H.

Hawke, Matthew, 46.
Hersey, William, 42, 69, 70.
Hersey, Dr. Ezekiel, 119—120.
Hersey, Rev. Henry, 136.
Hersey, Dr. Abner, 139—140.
Hilliard, Anthony, 47, 175.
Hills, Baker's, Otis's, 6.
Hingham, its situation, boundaries and extent, 5 ; annexed to Plymouth county, 5 ; surface, soil, productions, &c. 5—7 ; streams and ponds, 7 ; manufactures, trade, commerce, 7—8 ; population, 9 ; town expenses, 14, 89 ; education, 14—21 ; ecclesiastical history, 21—40 ; civil history, 40—113 ; longevity of inhabitants, 152, 157—158.
Hobart, Edmund, 69, 156.
Hobart, Thomas, 69.
Hobart, Joshua, 59—70, 79, 80.
Hobart, Rev. Peter, 21—25, 57—79, 156.
Hobart, Rev. Joshua, 113.
Hobart, Rev. Jeremiah, 113—114, 175.
Hobart, Rev. Gershom, 114—115.
Hobart, Japheth, 115.
Hobart, Rev. Nehemiah, 115.
Hobart, Rev. Noah, 117—118.

Hobart, Rev. Nehemiah of Cohasset, 34—35, 116.
Hobart, Dr. Peter, 90, 132.
Hobart families, sketch of 156—157.
Hotel, 8.
Houchin, Jeremiah, 163.
House lots, drawn, 22.
Huet, cure of one, 48.
Hull, Joseph, 44, 175.

I.

Ibbekin, Frederick Henry, 171—173.
Indian Deed, 159—162.
Indians, 80 ; orders against, 81, 84 ; incursions of, 83, 84.
Instructions to representatives, 81—82, 98—99, 106, 107.
Insurance Company, 10—11.
Islands, 7.

J.

Jacob, John deacon, 35.
Jacob, John slain by the Indians, 83.
Jefferson Debating Society, 12.
Joslin, Thomas, 49.
Joy, Thomas miller, 52—54.

K.

Kimball, Rev. Daniel, 19.

L.

Large, William, 43.
Leavitt, John his decendants, 44 ; see also Appendix, 175.
Leavitt, Jacob, 44.
Leavitt, Joshua, 44.
Leavitt, Dr. Martin, 130.
Lewis, Elijah, 90.
Lewis, Rev. Daniel, 116.
Lewis, Rev. Isaiah, 117.
Lewis, Joseph, 119.
Lewis, Thomas, 119.
Lewis, James, 120.
Libraries, 12—13.
Lincoln, Jeremiah, 90.
Lincoln, Hon. Levi, 90, 126—130.
Lincoln, Hon. Benjamin, 93.
Lincoln, Gen. Benjamin, 104, 105, 112, 140—146.
Lincoln, Enoch, 105, 106, 107, 148—149.
Lincoln, Isaac, 117.

Lincoln, Dr. Bela, 123—124.
Lincoln, Benjamin, 132.
Lincoln, Theodore, 133.
Lincoln, Rev. Henry, 133.
Lincoln, Abner, 19, 133—134.
Lincoln, Dr. Levi, 134,
Lincoln, Rev. Perez, 134.
Lincoln, Rev. Calvin, Jr. 136.
Lincoln, Solomon, Jr. 136.
Lincoln families, sketch of, 147—152.
Lincoln, Amos, 149.
Lincoln, Abraham, 149.
Lincoln, Mordecai, 149.
Lincoln, Thomas, weaver, 148.
Lincoln, Samuel, 148.
Lincoln, Thomas, cooper, 150.
Lincoln, Thomas, miller, 150.
Lincoln, Thomas, husbandman, 150.
Lincoln, Stephen, 151.
Lincoln, James Otis, 34, 150.
Lincolns, Longevity of, 152.
Lodge, Old Colony, 11, 12.
Loring, Thomas, 130.
Loring, Abner, 135.
Loring, Jerome, 135.
Loud, Jacob H. 136.
Ludkin, George, 43.
Ludkin, William, 45.

M.

Mackerel Fishery, 8, 9.
Marriages, in Gay's ministry, 30 ; in Ware's, 30.
Marsh, Thomas, 120.
Martin's Well, 43.
Meeting house new, 25 ; dispute respecting it, 85—87 ; at Glad Tidings Plain, 36.
Merrill Samuel, 19.
Methodists, 40.
Military difficulties, 55—79 ; 87—89.
Militia, 10, 89.
Mill, at the Cove, 52—54.
Mutual Aid, Society of, 11.

N.

Nantasket lands, controversy about, 53.
Newspaper, 12.
New England's Jonas, 74.

17

Norton, Rev. John, 24—25.
Norton, Andrews, 19, 134.
Norton, Elizabeth C. 19.
Nye, Cornelius, 117.

O.

Old Man's Calendar, 28—29.
Ordinary kept, 82.
Otis, John, 43 ; see also Appendix, 175.

P.

Payne, Stephen, 46.
Peck, Mr. Robert, 23.
Peck, Mr. Joseph, 45.
Pequod War, men furnished, 51.
Pine Tree Tavern, 43.
Pitts, Edmund, 45.
Poor, 13—14.
Pratt, Benjamin, 120—122.
Prince, Mr. Thomas, 25—26.
Proprietors' grant of lands to the town, 112.

R.

Record town, lost, 40.
Removal of inhabitants, 49.
Representatives, list of, 162—169.
Revolutionary proceedings, 91—112.
Rice, Caleb, 134.
Richardson, Rev. Joseph, 31, 137, 168.
Ripley, William, his descendants, 46.

S.

Salamander, a book entitled, 74.
Salary of ministers, 24, 25, 89.
Schoolmasters, 20—21.
Schools, 20—21.
Ship Yard, 8.
Shute, Rev. Daniel, 37, 108, 112.
Shute, Dr. Daniel, 132.
Shute, Dr. Daniel, Jr. 135, 137.
Smith, Henry, deacon, 23, 46.
Smith, Francis, 43.
Smith, Increase, S. 19.
Sprague, William, his descendants, 45.
Sprague, Knight, 90—91.
Stodder, Daniel, 158.
Stowers, Seth, 90.
Strong, John, 43.

Sutton, John, 46.

T.

Thaxter, Capt. Duncan, M. B. 10, 48.
Thaxter, Dr. Thomas, 32, 48.
Thaxter, Thomas, his descendants, 47—48.
Thaxter, Col. Samuel, 47.
Thaxter, Maj. Samuel, 48, 90, 123.
Thaxter, Dea. Joseph, 108.
Thaxter, Rev. Joseph, 108, 124—125.
Thaxter, Samuel, 116.
Thaxter, Samuel, another, 123.
Thaxter, Col. John, 123.
Thaxter, John, 130—132.
Thaxter, John, another, 135.
Thaxter, Dr. Robert, 134.
Tower, John, 49, 69.
Town Clerks, 169.
Town Meeting, when first held, 50.
Town orders, 50, 51, 52, 80, 81.

U.

Universalist Society, 40.

V.

Valuation of Hingham in 1749, 89—90.
Vassal, William, 74—75.
Vessels, permission to build, 8.
Voters, number of, 10.
Votes for Electors of President and Vice President, 112.
Votes for member of Congress, 112.
Votes for Governour, 170—171.

W.

Walton's Cove, 43.
Walton, William, 43, 175.
Ware, Rev. Henry, 30.
Ware, Rev. Henry, Jr. 135.
Ware, Dr. John, 135.
Ware, Rev. William, 136.
Waterman, Susan, 19.
Wear River, 7.
Weymouth Back River, 7.
Whitney, Rev. N. B. 37, 137.
Whiton, James, 49.
Wilder, James, H. 136.
Wilder families, sketch of, 153—155.
Woodward, Ralph, deacon, 23, 45.

www.ingramcontent.com/pod-product-compliance
Lightning Source LLC
Chambersburg PA
CBHW071425160426
43195CB00013B/1815